D1339625

PUBLIC CHOICE

PUBLIC CHOICE

Edited by

JULIEN VAN DEN BROECK

Professor of Economics,
Faculty of Applied Economics, University of Antwerp, Belgium

KLUWER ACADEMIC PUBLISHERS
DORDRECHT / BOSTON / LONDON

ASSOCIATION OF POST-KEYNESIAN STUDIES

HB
846.8
.P82
1988

Library of Congress Cataloging in Publication Data

Public choice / edited by Julien van den Broeck.
     p.   cm.
   A selection of papers presented at the annual conference of the
Association of Post-Keynesian Studies at the Erasmus University,
Rotterdam, the Netherlands, October 2, 1987.
   Includes bibliographies and indexes.
   ISBN 9024737672
   1. Social choice--Congresses.   I. Broeck, Julien van den, 1942-
. II. Association of Post-Keynesian Studies.
HB846.8.P82 1988
   302'.13--dc19   88-13174
                                                                 CIP

ISBN 90-247-3767-2

Published by Kluwer Academic Publishers,
P.O. Box 17, 3300 AA Dordrecht, The Netherlands.

Kluwer Academic Publishers incorporates
the publishing programmes of
D. Reidel, Martinus Nijhoff, Dr W. Junk and MTP Press.

Sold and distributed in the U.S.A. and Canada
by Kluwer Academic Publishers,
101 Philip Drive, Norwell, MA 02061, U.S.A.

In all other countries, sold and distributed
by Kluwer Academic Publishers,
P.O. Box 322, 3300 AH Dordrecht, The Netherlands.

Printed in The Netherlands

TABLE OF CONTENTS

Contributing Authors and Summary

The articles published in this book are the result of a selection of the papers presented at the annual conference of the Association of Post-Keynesian Studies at the Erasmus University, Rotterdam, the Netherlands, October 2, 1987.

As one of its major aims, the Association of Post-Keynesian Studies (APKS) encourages research covering various classic disciplines. Public choice theory is one of these research fields where several disciplines such as economics and political science meet and consequently is an apt theme for an APKS annual conference. Moreover APKS considers the investigation of the behaviour of governments in a modern economic setting to be of the utmost importance, because it can clarify the decision-making processes and the possible institutional factors which affect economic policies. Consequently, APKS is of opinion that the contributions in this book are of interest not only to Post-Keynesian economists but also to everybody dealing with governments in a professional way.

In the first contribution Frans A.A.M. van Winden (University of Amsterdam, Faculty of Economics, 1011 NH Amsterdam, the Netherlands) gives a survey of the public choice research field, which he describes as the economic theory of political decision-making. In his survey the author outlines the characteristics of public choice in the following way : (i) individualism is the point of departure, (ii) individuals strive after their own interests in a rational way and try to maximize utility, (iii) public choice uses methods and techniques of economic analysis and (iv) it has a preference for formalization, but he warns the reader that researchers are themselves involved in political processes, which can influence the outcome of their research. Van Winden goes on to analyse the behaviour of the various agents involved in the political decision-making process, i.e. voters, politicians, political parties, bureaucrats and interest groups, and he examines the studies dealing with so-called political economic models. Before putting the future development of public choice research into perspective, van Winden formulates a number of limitations and shortcomings (e.g. why do individuals vote at all ?, neglect of institutions, little attention to relationships between governmental bodies within a country or different countries, importance of social norms, etc....). The author concludes by indicating some major obstacles (e.g. the modelling of bargaining processes or pressure group activity) that have to be removed.

In his comments on van Winden's paper Jörg Glombowski (Tilburg University, Faculty of Economics, 5000 LE Tilburg, the Netherlands) points out that he has serious doubts about neoclassical economics and the applications of its methods in other fields. He finds bias in emphasis in public choice theory because it neglects the following facts : (i) many capitalist countries are not democracies, (ii) present-day democratic institutions are fairly young and (iii) the stability of the capitalist-democratic "marriage" is not guaranteed. Concerning the motivations (income, power, prestige) of politicians the author is convinced that these are not specific to them. Glombowski agrees with van Winden's proposition of group-related interest function but he is afraid that microfundamentalists will consider this as "ad hoc-theorizing". After pointing out the enormous institutional variety the author makes it clear that the exercise of political power is restricted. He argues that the opposition is not powerless because it has its adherents appointed by former governments and there are social and economic pressure groups which can restrict the power of politicians. Glombowski concludes by making some critical remarks especially about the assumptions of voting behaviour and stressing the importance to be given to old-fashioned interdisciplinary contacts.

In the second section of this book Vani K Borooah (University of Ulster, Faculty of Business and Management, Newtownabbey Co. Antrim, BT 37 0QB Northern Ireland, United Kingdom) attempts to examine the interaction between events in the political and economic spheres and the role of such interaction in determining macroeconomic policy. He indicates that the proposition that a government's macroeconomic policies and the results of those policies significantly affect its electoral popularity is not without support but that it is not clear which economic factors really affect this relationship. The author points out that stability analysis and differences in voter self-interest are relatively neglected in this field, which seriously biases the results. Borooah goes on to investigate the possibility that macroeconomic policy has been manipulated by politicians in order to secure their political advantage. He discusses the literature on this theme and points out that neither Marx nor Kalecki were strangers to the idea that the functioning of an economy has a political basis. They viewed class conflict between capitalists and workers, with the government aiding the capitalist class and the workers attempting to restrict its ability to do so, as the regulator of the interaction between economics and politics. Unfortunately, stresses V. K Borooah, the importance of social conflict has been ignored by mainstream economics which has instead sought to situate the interaction between economics and politics within the narrow confines of electoral behaviour. He concludes by attempting to demonstrate that the notion of conflict when applied to inter-ministerial conflict can to a certain extent explain the rise in public expenditure in the United Kingdom.

Dirk Heremans (Catholic University of Leuven, Center for Economic Studies, 3000 Leuven, Belgium) comments in his paper on the relationship, as described by Borooah, between public choice theory and macroeconomic policy. The author proposes to adopt an alternative approach where macroeconomic model building incorporates public choice theory elements instead of the other way around, which has been labelled "credibility and politics". In explaining this new approach as a game between policy makers and private agents in the economy he emphasizes the important role of political institutions as well as the interaction between short-sighted politicians and long-sighted political parties. As a result of this approach it seems that investing in its reputation by a government will be a determining factor in its policy effectiveness and electoral success. Heremans goes on to point out that more fragmented horizontal redistribution schemes may be more relevant than simple class conflict between capitalists and workers. In particular, governments themselves are playing a more independent role. Therefore one can ask whether it is not more important to investigate how institutions filter out pressures and conflicts as well as how they regulate the outcomes of them. Commenting on public expenditure and the organization of the budgetary process the author argues in favour of adopting a more disaggregating approach by investigating the relation between central and local government instead of concentrating on central government alone. Heremans concludes that the manipulation of macroeconomic policies by governments will depend on the political institutions as well as on their reputation.

In part three the managerial analysis of public investment policies is highlighted by Alain Verbeke (University of Antwerp (RUCA), Faculty of Applied Economics, 2020 Antwerpen, Belgium and University of Toronto, International Business Center, Toronto, M5S 1Y4 Canada). In his article he investigates in depth the issue of investment processes whereby no actor is deemed directly responsible for the production activities, i.e. the allocation of financial resources "à fonds perdus", and points out that such a situation occurs very often with investments in the public infrastructure sphere. Because traditional investment analysis or project evaluation with public investment are mostly used to justify specific choices, already made by decision makers and because, according to classic public choice theory, self-interest is one of its main premises, it seems quite natural to the author that the mere introduction of an analytical tool will not change this investment behaviour. Therefore, Verbeke proposes to develop a new theoretical framework to tackle the problem of investment processes financed with resources allocated "à fonds perdus". Before developing this framework Verbeke first discusses the issue of effectiveness of investment processes. He also points out that he - in contrast to other authors - adopts a selective rationality approach i.e. dismissing the premise of maximizing behaviour by bureaucrats or politicians, with respect to effectiveness analysis. The author further discusses the effectiveness issue with respect to the normative theory of welfare economics (cost-benefit analysis) and the transaction cost theory, indicating that the latter is based upon bounded ratinality and opportunism. As a result he proposes to assess the effectiveness of resource allocation processes by using various analysis models (multiple perspective approach). Verbeke starts discussing the normative rational objectives model by indicating its boundaries and giving the model a comparative institutional interpretation. He further argues that the rational objectives model provides an effective governance structure and can be used as a prescriptive policy instrument. However, one can question the existence of a strategic level with this model and it does not explain the existence of ineffectiveness. Therefore, the author introduces the structural ineffectiveness model. Inertia (non-elimination of observed ineffectiveness) is the key-word of this model. He explains why inertia exists and how it could be removed and how ineffectiveness could be reduced ("delegation" to a higher authority, exogenous pressure or bad results and internal control) Verbeke goes on, however, to point out that these models cannot be used to analyze investment decisions in an organized anarchy (i.e. objectives as a guideline do not exist or, if they do, they are neither controlled nor completely understood and the activity levels cannot be precisely determined). Therefore, he develops a third model, i.e. the commitment model, which is very close to the traditional public choice theory, because this model considers public investments as a result of political transactions. After the application of the various models to Belgian seaport policy with respect to infrastructural investment projects Verbeke concludes that, although the results are contradictory, the multiple perspective approach is very appropriate for tackling the extremely complex "à fonds perdus" allocation problem with public infrastructure investment.

Julien van den Broeck

PART ONE:
PUBLIC CHOICE: THE STATE OF THE ART

1 THE ECONOMIC THEORY OF POLITICAL DECISION-MAKING :
A Survey and Perspective

Frans A.A.M. van Winden

1.1. Introduction

The economic theory of political decision-making is concerned with the determinants and effects of decision-making in the political sphere of a society. This sphere is generally considered to be determined by those agents and their relationships that are of direct importance for the way governments behave; where governments as organizations are distinguished from other agents by their successful claim, within a certain territory, of a monopoly of legitimate physical force (cf. Weber, 1972, (1922)). Studies pertaining to the subject at hand often have a strongly multi-disciplinary flavour due to the interface with, especially, political science and law. The desirable unification of - at least some of - the social sciences seems to be particularly advanced in this field of research, which is alternatively labelled as modern political economy, public choice or political economics. The term modern political economy is reminiscent of the fact that the study of government behaviour was, to some extent at least, integrated into classical economics (Smith, Mill, Marx), when economics was still called political economy. The so-called marginal (neoclassical) revolution in the latter half of the 19th century entailed that attention became increasingly focused on the behaviour of individual (consumers, entrepreneurs) and the functioning of atomistic markets with no leeway for the participants to influence their outcome. Problems of power and bargaining - which are central to the analysis of political decision-making - did not fit into this research program.

Julien van den Broeck (ed.), Public Choice, 9-42.
© *1988 by Kluwer Academic Publishers and Association of Post-Keynesian Studies.*

Although the development of welfare economics (the theory of public goods) and of macro-economics after World-War II did much to increase the attention of economists for the effects of government behaviour, the analysis of its determinant was left to others. Even today it is probably fair to say that by and large economists are not very much interested in how political decisions are reached. The dominant (normative) approach is in terms of what governments should do instead of what they actually do (positive approach), which is in sharp contrast with the usual positive approach of consumer and producer behaviour in the market sector. Market failures, judged by the criteria of (Pareto-)efficiency and equity, are typically considered to be a necessary condition for government intervention. Because of the importance of government policies for the allocation of 'scarce means which have alternative uses' - the essential ingredient of the subject-matter of economic analysis as traditionally defined - this state of affairs implied a serious lacuna in mainstream economic theory. And, although a positive approach of government behaviour is characteristic of Marxian economics, students following this tradition of economic thought have not been able to fill the gap. Even within the tradition itself the development of the theory of the state has not made very much progress (cf. van Winden, 1983).

After World-War II, and especially during the last two decades, an increasing number of economists got attracted to this neglected field of research that became widely known as public choice, in particular through the inspiring and thought-provoking works and other professional efforts of Buchanan and Tullock (the latter is senior editor of the journal Public Choice). The awarding of the 1986 Nobel Prize in Economics to Buchanan gives expression, and support, to the acknowledgement of the relevance and importance of work in this area, and can be expected to stimulate its further development. From a methodological point of view public choice can be characterized in the following way :

1. methodological individualism as point of departure;
2. the assumption that individuals (a) strive after their own interests, (b) in a rational way, and (c) try to maximize utility; this assumption may be called the fundamental behavioural hypothesis of public choice;

and, further:

3. the use of methods and techniques of economic analysis;
4. a preference for formalization (quantitative analysis), if compared with the Marxian theory of the state.

The first two characteristics put public choice within the tradition of neoclassical economics. The essential aspect here is that the applicability of the neoclassical assumptions is extended from the market sector to the political sphere. The basic idea is that a priori there seems to be no reason to expect that the motives of individuals in these two sectors differ. Only the environment in which they act is different, enforcing different kinds of restrictions upon the realization of their interests.

Before going into the achievements and themes that are on the research agenda of public choice I would like to indicate a problem that, although also being encountered elsewhere in the social sciences, seems to be particularly acute here. The problem is that the nature of the subject-matter of study at hand is such that it may hamper an objective analysis. Because of the involvement of individuals (including researchers) in political processes, the importance of information as a determinant of behaviour, and given the special position of governments within societies (see above), it should not surprise us that from time to time ideologies and strategic behaviour - that is, taking account of the political effects of research - leave their traces. The fact that public choice is sometimes associated with rightist political movements is not without substance. It is among the reasons why some people, especially in Europe it seems, prefer the term 'modern political economy' or 'political economics'.

In the following section I will give a concise survey of research themes and the results obtained. Given the space constraints, I have to be selective here and restrict myself to some main points (more extensive surveys are presented in: Frey, 1978a; Mueller, 1979; Van den Doel, 1979). The ensuing section discusses some limitations and shortcomings of the research undertaken. In the final section the state of the art will be brought into perspective against the background of this critique.

1.2. Themes and results

In this section a synopsis is presented of the major research topics that have been studied and of the theoretical and empirical results obtained. As noted above the methods and techniques thereby employed are typically taken from the economist's tool-box, covering the whole range from elementary to highly advanced mathematical economics (including game theory) and econometrics. Space does not allow me to go into details here.

As regards the research themes a - for the sake of exposition - fruitful distinction can be made between studies that analyze the more or less isolated behaviour of the different agents involved in the political decision-making process - to wit: voters, politicians, political parties, bureaucrats, pressure groups - and studies concerned with the interaction between the public (government) sector and the private (market) sector in an economy, the so-called political economic models.

a.   Voters.

As almost exlusively societies with a political system of a democratic nature are studied it is not surprising that voting behaviour - consisting of a decision to vote or to abstain and a choice of party (candidate) in case of the former - plays an important role in the analysis. Following Downs (1957), this behaviour - as exhibited in actual elections or popularity polls - is typically related to the utility change that voters expect from voting for a particular candidate or party instead of another one or abstention from voting.

There are many theoretical issues involved here. For example, what sort of information do voters use? Do they focus on the extent to which their (economic) interests have been realized under the recent - and, possibly, past - governments, holding the latter ultimately responsibly for this ('retrospective voting'), or do they take account of political platforms and future effects of government policies ('prospective' or 'strategic' voting)? Are personal circumstances determinant ('pocketbook voting') or national economic developments ('sociotropic voting'), or something in between? How to allow for party-identification? In case of multiparty-systems, do voters, under the responsibility hypothesis, hold coalition parties equally responsible? What sort of choice model should be employed, which (economic) variables should be used as arguments in the utility function, and which specification should be chosen for the latter? Is it acceptable to use exactly the same model for all voters or, else, how to distinguish between groups of voters?

In empirical work voter turnout (the decision to vote) has typically been related to the change in utility (benefits) expected by a voter if the most favourite choice of party wins, and the perceived probability that one's vote is decisive in this respect. In addition, benefits ('civic duty' fulfilment) and costs (time spent) derived from voting per se are taken account of. As regards party choice, the vote share or popularity (in case of polls) of parties has generally been related to the level or growth rate of some macroeconomic variables - in particular the unemployment rate, the growth rate of national income and the rate of inflation - in the past ('retrospective voting'), while party-identification and myopia (discounting of past events) are allowed for by the introduction of, respectively, a constant term and the previous vote share (popularity) in the vote (popularity) function.

As yet, research on party choice has turned out to be much more successful than that on voter turnout. The upshot of this research is that economic conditions do seem to play a role, that governments are apparently held responsible for them, and that voters are myopic as they particularly seem to focus on economic conditions in the near past. A notorious problem, however, is that the empirical relationships are very unstable; they are often sensitive, for example, to the length of the observation period (cf. Paldam, 1981). Referring to the theoretical issues mentioned above, this may be due to an incorrect formalization of the choice process (most vote and popularity functions even lack a rigorous theoretical underpinning), the fact that no allowance is made for prospective or strategic voting, the use of objective economic indicators instead of perceptions, the influence of omitted variables which may for example be responsible for shifts in party-identification, or the general assumption that voters can be considered as a homogeneous group. Although these issues have received some attention in the empirical literature - including the special problem of multiparty systems (cf. Renaud and van Winden, 1987) - there is a need for studies that treat them in an integrative and systematic way. It should be noted, however, that a serious lack of adequate data often stands in the way here.

As earlier indicated, the explanation of voter turnout has been less successful. Although there is evidence that voter participation is positively related to the closeness of elections (see Mueller, 1979, p. 123), the relationship as such can hardly be reconciled with the assumption of rational voting behaviour as the probability of one's voting being decisive will in reality always be infinitesimally small in large-scale elections, evoking free-rider behaviour. Another empirical result worth mentioning is the systematic finding that bureaucrats show a relatively higher turnout than other social groups (cf. Jaarsma et al., 1986). It lends further support to the suspicion that the electorate should not be treated as homogeneous. By distinguishing between social groups it may further become possible to reconcile the empirical finding that whereas personal circumstances do not appear to be as important as general economic conditions for voting behaviour, the impact of the latter is highly unstable. As it is unlikely that distributional aspects do not count at all, but, on the other hand, plausible that political decision-makers cannot (due to information costs) or will not take account of circumstances on a purely individual level (due to a lack of political influence on that level), it seems more likely that voters focus on the welfare of representative individuals of social reference groups. I will return to this later on.

b. Politicians. The basic assumption is that politicians - elected representatives - are motivated by their self-interest which is seen to be the income, power and prestige derived from being in office (Downs, 1957). In order to reap these benefits it is necessary to be (re-)elected. According to Downs politicians will therefore formulate policies in order to win elections, rather than do the reverse; an assumption which at least goes back to Schumpeter (1947). This leads to the hypothesis that politicians try to maximize the number of voters, a hypothesis that is still often maintained. Related hypotheses are the maximization of (expected) plurality, the vote share or the probability of winning. Which policies politicians should choose to that purpose will in general depend on the preference structure of society, its political influence structure (cf. campaign contributions, for example), the character of the party that is represented (e.g., the strength of the party-line), the relationship with the bureaucracy that has to implement such policies, and the behaviour of other politicians (parties). Research in this area has been concentrated on the relationship between politicians and voters, neglecting the importance of the other factors mentioned, in particular by (implicitly) assuming that parties and governments are homogeneous entities (teams) with no internal conflicts of interests and that political influence is restricted to voting.

Most popular in this context is the 'median voter model' (for some other models, see below). Suppose that voters have single-peaked preferences regarding the alternatives in case of a one-dimensional issue, such as the share of public expenditure in national income. This means that there is one most preferred alternative while the further another alternative is removed from it the less attractive the latter will be. Suppose further that voters wil vote for the alternative that is closest to the most preferred one (rationality). In that case majority voting, with no abstention, will select the alternative that is most preferred by the median voter, which is located on the median of the frequency distribution of most preferred alternatives (that is, at least 50% of the other voters prefers the same or a smaller expenditure share and at least 50% the same or a higher share) ; the possibility of a tie is here neglected. This would suggest that parties (politicians) - at any rate in the mostly studied case of a two-party system - will be pulled towards the middle of the political spectrum, choosing policies in line with the preferences of the median voter.

There are many empirical applications of the median voter model. In these studies median income and the median tax share are used to operationalize the concept of a median voter. One of the more interesting studies from a theoretical point of view is Pommerehne (1978), where the model is applied to Swiss municipalities, some of which can be characterized as direct democracies while others are of a representative kind. The results of this study suggest that the demand-oriented median voter model is better fit for democracies with referenda than for representative democracies with no referenda. Furthermore, for direct democracies the model produces far better results than a 'traditional' model with average income and the average tax share, which does not take account of institutional aspects of political economic decision-making. For representative democracies supply-side factors such as the influence of the bureaucracy appeared to be important. All in all, the empirical results obtained with median voter models are inconclusive. Moreover, they have been strongly criticized from a methodological and theoretical point of view (Bergstrom and Goodman, 1973; Romer and Rosenthal, 1979). Apart from some econometric problems which leave, for example, the importance of median income versus other income levels and the expenditure level most preferred by the median voter in doubt, it has to be concluded that the model is unfit for application to representative democracies for a large number of reasons. First, the decisiveness of the median voter generally only holds for majority-voting regarding a one-dimensional issue (cf. Enelow and Hinich, 1984). Second, the model generally only applies to situations in which all voters vote (no abstention). Third, it is assumed that the participants are fully informed with respect to the relevant aspects of decision-making. The differential impact of information costs on political participation - which makes it interesting for politicians and parties to focus on particular social groups (producers instead of consumers, for example; see Downs, 1957) - and, to mention another point, the myopia of voters suggested by studies on voting behaviour are neglected. Fourth, the fact that elections are only held at regular time-intervals gives an opportunity to self-interested politicians to deviate from the preferences of a median voter, and the more so if voters are indeed myopic. Fifth, it cannot be excluded that politicians (parties), as monopolistic suppliers of public goods, will collude instead of fighting each other for votes (especially, in case of a two-party system; cf. Wittman, 1973). Sixth, the assumption that politicians and parties want to win elections at all costs, since they would be powerless when in the opposition, seems too strong, and even more so the assumption that they strive after (some form of) vote maximization. As regards the latter a more plausible assumption would seem to be that they care for a sufficient vote share at election time (cf.: Breton, 1974; Frey and Lau, 1968), and regarding the former the assumption that political influence is a more or less smoothly increasing function of the size of a party (cf. Stigler, 1972). Such assumptions direct attention to the interests (utility, ideology) of politicians and the parties they represent, and consequently also to the nature of the relationship between these two. As yet public choice models of the behaviour of politicians employing such more realistic assumptions, while satisfying the claim of methodological individualism, are lacking, however. Seventh, it is unrealistic to neglect all other forms of political participation than voting; for example, the influence of bureaucrats on government policies, as indicated in Pommerehne's study and strongly emphasized elsewhere in the public choice literature (see below). Finally, it is noticed that the assumption of a homogeneous government - even when parties could be considered as such - cannot be maintained in case of multi-party systems with coalition governments. Moreover, due to the complexities of coalition formation it is not at all clear then which vote-share is required for membership in a coalition.

c.   Political parties.   As noted above, in public choice models often no distinction is made between politicians and political parties. They are typically assumed to have the same goals (team assumption). However, especially from the point of view of methodological individualism, it should be acknowledged that: (a) politicians operate at some distance of the parties they represent (they are in a different position in the political decision-making process) which directs attention to the importance of the party-line; (b) upward mobility within parties is restricted, implying that for most members the chance of ever becoming a politician is probably negligible; (c) the general empirical observation of fractions or wings in parties brings to the fore the existence of internal conflicts of interests. Up till now only a very few models have been developed that take such issues into account. An example, within the context of the median voter model, is Coleman (1971) where party candidates have to compete for nomination within and among parties. The result is that they will generally choose a position between the median of the party and that of the electorate.

Apart from the way conflicting interests within parties are compromised, some attention has been paid to such elements of party behaviour as campaign spending and its effect on votes, and the provision of information (see Mueller, 1979, pp.117-120). As regards the latter it is expected that parties will tend to choose a median position and an ambiguous stand with respect to issues for which voters have little incentive to become well informed (in particular those concerning the allocation of public goods due to the free-rider problem) and a much clearer minority position regarding redistributional issues that are of special interest for minority groups, for which the latter have an incentive to gather information (in particular those related to their source of income or geographical area). This may lead to overexpenditure on special interest legislation and underexpenditure on general interest legislation.

The behaviour of parties vis-à-vis other parties, and the nature of its outcome (stability, efficiency), has been generally studied within the framework of a spatial model, where the parties are taken to compete for votes in a policy space spanned by one or more issue dimensions along which the preferences of voters are distributed in a given way. Not surprisingly, these models have run into similar problems as were met with the median voter model. Thus, for example, in case of a multi-dimensional policy space and a two-party system, it is required for stability (that is, a policy that cannot be beaten) that some very stringent conditions with respect to voter preferences are satisfied, which in essence demand that voters are more or less alike (Kramer, 1973). As there seems to be a lot more stability than suggested by those models, in recent research attentions, interalia, paid to the importance of imperfect information (uncertainty) and institutional constraints inthis context (cf.: Coughlin and Nitzan, 1981; Shepsly, 1979; Wittman, 1987).

Analytical complexities increase dramatically with multi-party systems, especially in case of coalition governments (see Holler,1987). In order to allow for coalitions one has to solve the problem of their membership as well as the problem of what the payoffs - in terms of cabinet portfolio's and policies - will be. The nature of these problems obviously sugests the use of game theory, which is indeed often employed. Most theoretical analysis and empirical applications are thereby concerned with the membership issue. The distribution of payoffs - particularly regarding policies - has been subject of much less (empirical) work (Laver, 1985; Schofield and Laver, 1987). With respect to coalition formation one very popular hypothesis has been that of the 'minimum winning coalition' (Riker, 1962), which says that only those coalitions will form that exclude parties whose weight is unnecessary for the coalition to be winning, that is to satisfy a majority criterion so that it can form the cabinet. Politics is considered to be a zero-sum game, here. Empirically, this hypothesis has been found to be inferior to the so-called 'minimal connected winning coalition' hypothesis put forward in Axelrod (1970) which suggests that parties with less 'conflict of interests' (ideological diversity, as measured on a Left-Right scale, for example) will join to form a winning coalition. Parties that bridge ideological 'gaps' will be contained in such a coalition even though they may make the coalition larger in size than necessary (see: De Swaan, 1973; Taylor and Laver, 1973). A satisfactory theoretical underpinning of this hypothesis is lacking, however. There are also still unresolved problems with the explanation of minority coalitions and super (non-minimal) coalitions which quite often appear to occur.

Other issues addressed are, for example, the effects of electoral systems - such as a plurality system versus a proportional system - on the relationship between votes and parliamentary seats (as well as between the latter and cabinet posts), the stability of coalitions in terms of their duration (there is evidence that coalitions do not necesarily perform worse in this respect compared with majority party systems), the policy shocks produced by government changes (it is suggested that heavier shocks are produced under two-party systems), the possibility of strategic voting, and the conditions for rational voting (see Holler,1987). Little attention has been given as yet to the dynamics of party systems, in particular the demise and formation of parties. The nature of the electoral system is considered to be important in this respect. Plurality systems, for example, are generally considered to be conducive to the rise of a two-party system. According to Riker's 'minimum winning coalition' hypothesis there would even be a general tendency towards such a system, also in case of a proportional system. In a dynamic context, furthermore, the common assumption that voters' preferences are given becomes doubtful as parties and politicians may have instruments to change them (think of the promotion of people's capitalism). Finally, it is mentioned here that coalition formation models do not incorporate any model of voting behaviour, which seems strange as parties are made up by voters (see van Winden, 1983).

d. Bureaucrats. The most influential hypothesis regarding the behaviour of bureaucrats to date, put forward in Niskanen (1971), is that they will try to maximize their budgets. The hypothesis strongly contrasts with the traditional view - stimulated by the work of Max Weber - of a docile and subservient government work force.

Niskanen derived his hypothesis from the assumption of self-interested bureaucrats and the nature of the environment in which they operate. As regards the latter, the lack of information with politicians to adequately monitor their performance is crucial. There is a serious information problem with respect to the benefits of many of the activities that they perform (think of the preference revelation problem in the context of public goods) as well as regarding the necessary costs of these activities. The second problem is due to the fact that bureaucrats are often monopolistic suppliers of the goods and services they produce giving them expert knowledge which is reinforced by the on average relatively short stay of elected politicians in the government organization. The result is that bureaucrats have some leeway to promote their own interests. The question then becomes what these interests or goals are. Although they ultimately cover a wide variety of monetary and non-monetary items - such as salary, power, perquisites of the office, reputation, output, and an easy life - most of them are in Niskanen's view related to the size of the budget appropriated to them by the politicians; whence his hypothesis. The upshot of this model is that output is produced against minimum cost (technical efficiency), but in larger amount than optimal for the politicians or the population whose interests they represent (marginal costs exceed the marginal benefits). Although output maximization is a goal that has also been imputed in the organization literature to the managers of large corporations (cf. Orzechowski, 1977), the assumption is not strongly motivated by Niskanen. It should further be noticed that production against minimum cost implies that no surplus is left for the salary and perquisites that bureaucrats assumedly are interested in . This had led Migué and Bélanger (1974) to formulate a model in which bureaucrats are supposed to have a preference for output as well as budget surplus (discretionary budget). The result is that cost minimization no longer occurs, so that now technical inefficiency along with a budget (output level) that is too large from the politicians' point of view arises. There is indeed empirical evidence which suggests that production costs in the public sector are higher than they would be in the private sector (e.g., Orzechowski, 1977). With respect to the technology choice of production it has further been suggested in the literature that production will not only be inefficient but in addition labour-input biased; empirical support for this proposition is given in Orzechowski (1977).

The state of the art of research in this area is such that as yet no convincing and comprehensive model of bureaucratic behaviour exists. The issues involved are highly complex. One important problem, for example, is the effect of mobility and competition within and across bureaus. According to Breton and Wintrobe (1982, p. 9) this may even lead to the result that each information distorting bureau à la Niskanen - and hence the bureaucracy - would be too small rather than too large. Also bureaucrats may prefer to be promoted to a (possibly smaller) bureau higher up in the hierarchy instead of trying to expand their present bureau. In this respect, it is important to note that politicians may have more means available to check bureaucratic behaviour than suggested by Niskanen's model. Activities of bureaus may overlap, for example, or meet competition from private suppliers.

A more satisfying comprehensive interactive model of the supply of and demand for government goods and services, should not only allow for the afore mentioned aspects which refer to the relationship between bureaucrats and politicians, but would also have to take account of the impact of outside pressure groups - including political parties - on bureaucratic behaviour (see, e.g., Friedman, 1984, pp. 348 ff.). Moreover, it should take account of the fact that bureaucrats may indirectly influence governmental decision-making as voters (recall their higher turnout level in elections), by becoming a member of parliament and by participating in pressure group activity. Empirical studies suggest that these opportunities are also extensively used (see, e.g., van Winden, 1987).

Such a wider perspective on supply and demand factors may, furthermore, contribute to the debate whether there is indeed an oversupply (Downs) of government goods and services.

e. <u>Interest groups</u>. Although it is generally acknowledged that interest groups trying to influence political decision-making are extremely important for the explanation of government behaviour, their behaviour has been studied the least systematic. This is no doubt to a large extent due to the complexities of bargaining (cf. government coalition formation) inherent in this research subject, as well as to the lack of adequate data.

Analytically, a distinction can be made between two types of problems here : (a) the determinants of the formation of interests groups; and (b) the way they influence political decision-making.

Regarding the first problem a pioneering and highly influential study is Olson ((1965). The central point that Olson wants to make is that, as an interest group is defined by a common interest for the members of the group that they try to realize through collective action, free-riding may stand in the way of the formation of such a group due to the public good aspects that are involved. In case of a small group this problem may be overcome because of the non-negligeable impact of the behaviour of each single member on the group outcome and the better opportunities for monotoring each other's activities and the enforcement of social norms. In case of a large group - such a union or consumer organization - selective incentives (with a private good character) or coercion will be needed, however, according to Olson. A number of implications that he infers from his 'logic of collective action' are discussed in Olson (1982). For example, it is argued that countries will not show a symmetrical organization of all groups with a common interest. Some groups such as consumers, tax payers, the unemployed and the poor are said to miss the selective incentives or the small numbers needed to organize. Olson also infers that stable societies are conducive to the accumulation of interest groups over time. Furthermore, it is argued that such groups will be oriented to the redistribution of income and wealth - an activity which has been labelled 'rent seeking' elsewhere in the public choice literature (see Tollison, 1982) - rather than the production of additional output (unless they are so-called encompassing organizations). Olson expects that such 'distributional coalitions' will slow down economic growth and increase the complexity of regulation and the role of government.

Some supportive empirical evidence for Olson's theory of interest group formation is presented in Murrell (1984). It appears that the length of time since modern political and economic development in a country began is indeed important, as well as the size of the population and the extent of decentralization of government. Similar results are reported by Mueller and Murrel (1986).

With respect to the second type of problem - i.e., the way that interest groups influence political decision-making - a distinction can be made between means, behaviour and results (cf. the triple: structure, conduct and performance, in the industrial organization literature). Politically important means available to interest groups may be: information, such as on the preferences of their constituencies; money, for campaign contributions, for example (cf. the Political Action Committees in the U.S.); or means to influence the economy - such as work or investment strikes - through which government policies may be hindered, tax revenues affected, and voter attitudes changed (see Gärtner, 1981).

There are only very few studies that explicitly deal with the behaviour of interest groups. An interesting theoretical study is Becker (1983). In this study interest groups obtain - purely redistributive - political influence through the production of political pressure. Subsidies are distributed and financed out of taxes. Because of transaction costs and efficiency costs (due to adverse incentive effects of taxes and subsidies) the total tax sum exceeds the total of the subsidies, however. In equilibrium the pressure to increase subsidies just equals the pressure to reduce taxes, while the marginal costs of pressure equals its marginal benefit. Remarkably, it appears from Becker's analysis that political policies that raise efficiency are more likely to be adopted than policies that lower efficiency. Thus, interest groups that are cheap to subsidize or expansive to tax would do better, for example. Although this model is to be regarded as a first approach linking government policies to interest group behaviour, as other political decision-makers (politicians, bureaucrats, parties, voters) do not play an independent role, it is an important first step.

Empirical studies concerning the political influence of interest groups generally focus on the relationship between means and results (structure and performance), leaving out the behaviour (conduct) that is in between. Most of them are case studies concentrating on a specific sector of the economy and some specific political benefits. Salamon and Siegfried (1977), for example, consider the distribution of the effective federal corporation income tax rates across industries in the U.S. The hypothesis that this distribution will be related to the structure of the different industries in terms of firm size, industry size, concentration rate, etc., as these characteristics assumedly tell something about free-rider problems, resources and incentives. Their results show a significant positive influence of firm size only. Frey (1984, p. 58) summarizes empirical studies concerned with the unequal degree of protection among industries against foreign competition. His conclusion is that tariffs and non-tariff barriers are positively linked to the importance and degree of concentration of import-competing industries. Declining industries, and sectors with low-skilled, low-wage employees in large numbers appear to have a good chance of getting protection.

Esty and Caves (1983) indicate three shortcomings of this type of studies. First, attention is focussed on a single outcome of political influence only (such as tariffs). Second, the locus of political decisions is generally obscure. Third, the role of expenditures in yielding political influence is neglected. In their study they try to remedy these shortcomings by observing the bills introduced in the U.S. Congress, during a particular time-interval, which are deemed to affect the specific interests of a sample of industries. Also, information is secured from the industries' lobbying organizations on their legislative priorities during these years and how many goals they achieved. Regarding expenditures it is investigated whether they perform an independent role (irrespective the type of spending industry) or a facilitating role. In the latter case political expenditures represent a transaction cost needed to convert an industry's structural attributes into effective influence. The statistical results appear to confirm both roles for expenditure, which suggests a serious weakness of the structure-performance approach which neglects political acitivity. Moreover, it turns out - in contrast with Salamon and Siegfried's study - that the concentration rate and geographic dispersion increase both activity and success, whereas neither firm size nor industry size proves to be significant.

Most of the empirical studies on the political influence of interest groups are concerned with outcomes of regulation which redistribute income indirectly. Empirical support for their influence on direct income transfers has recently been reported in Plotnick (1986), however.

Finally, it is mentioned that as regards the impact of interest groups on the relative size of the government sector the empirical results in Mueller and Murrell (1986), obtained from a cross-section of OECD countries, suggest that the number of such groups in a country has a significantly positive effect.

The relationships between interest group activity and government growth, and between the latter and macroeconomic performance, is still largely unexplored, however (cf. Mueller, 1987, p. 133).

f. <u>Political economic models</u>.   Models thus labelled are meant to formalize the interaction between government decision-making and the functioning of the economy. Up till now attention has generally been focused on the relationship between consumer-voters and the government (in particular, incumbent politicians). According to Frey (1978b, p. 203) one of the pioneers in this field :"The basic idea of a polico-economic model is that the voters' evaluation of government performance, and therefore a government's chance of staying in power, depend substanstially on economic conditions; and that the government in turn seeks to manipulate the economy in order to stay in power and to maximize its utility (e.g., by putting ideological programs into action)".
Stimulated by Nordhaus (1975) a large part of this literature has been concerned with the so-called political business cycle, which is a cycle in economic activity caused by political decision-making. Nordhaus showed the possibility of such a cycle using a model which is essentially

based on the following assumptions: (a) the government tries to maximize the (expected) number of votes at the forthcoming election, as the incumbent politicians assumedly want to secure their re-election; (b) voters negatively value unemployment and inflation, hold the government responsible for these economic outcomes, and are retrospective and more or less myopic in judging the government's (imputed) performance in this respect; (c) the goverment is able to manipulate unemployment and inflation along a Phillips-curve representing a negative relationship between these two variables, with inflation expectations gradually adjusting to the unemployment rate observed. Under these assumptions the government will bring down the unemployment rate before the election date, exploiting the lagged response of inflation, while causing an increase in unemployment afterwards in order to fight the rise of inflation and to obtain a favourable position for the next election round. A host of publications followed Nordhaus' seminal study, investigating the theoretical conditions under which a political business cycle is generated and/or its empirical relevance (see, e.g., Borooah and Van der Ploeg, 1983; Hibbs and Fassbender, 1981). The general conclusion seems to be that there is no strong empirical evidence for its existence.

One of the problems is that economic outcomes instead of the government's use of its instruments is often focussed upon. A more interesting model of government behaviour in this respect, as well as one that is better fit for incorporation in a full-fledged macro-economic model, is that developed by Frey and Schneider (see Frey, 1978b). It has the following characteristics; (1) as in Nordhaus' model attention is concentrated on the relationship between self-interested incumbent politicians and voters; political parties are taken to share the interests of the politicians by which they are represented; (2) the interests of voters are represented by a popularity function, in which the unemployment rate, the rate of inflation and the macro-economic growth rate of real disposable income figure as arguments; (3) in contrast with Downs (1975), it is assumed that politicians (parties) try to maximize a utility function - instead of the number of votes - where utility is related to the realization of ideological goals, operationalized by assuming that leftist (rightist) parties strive after a higher (lower) share of government expenditure in national income; (4) as incumbency is supposed to be a necessary condition for the realization of ideological goals (politicians are considerd powerless when in opposition) politicians will try to manipulate the macro-economic variables appearing in the popularity function when they expect a popularity deficit (as shown by the polls), in order to satisfy the re-election constraint; (5) apart from this constraint on the behaviour of politicians - which is deemed to be most crucial economic and administrative constraints are taken into account; as regards the former it is pointed at the budget constraint, for example, while regarding the latter it is hypothesized that bureaucrats will only allow gradual (incremental) changes in the policy instruments such as goverment consumption, investment and transfers (the relationship between instrument use and government goals is called the reaction of policy function). From empirical applications to the U.S., the U.K. and the Federal Republic of Germany, and comparisons with other models (among which a traditional macro-economic model with an exogenous government), Frey and Schneider conclude that their model renders a fairly good approximation of reality. More particularly, in case of a popularity deficit both leftist and rightist governments would seem to step up expenditure in order to increase popularity, while in case of an expected popularity surplus leftist governments show an inclination towards higher expenditure levels than right-wing governments. In line with the administrative constraint assumption, expenditures appear to be strongly related to previous expenditure levels.

The critique on this model runs in the following directions. First, the different variants of the model used are not completely consistent. Second, as noted earlier, estimates of popularity functions have been shown to be notariously unstable. Third, the behaviour of important actors is neglected (other governments, pressure groups) or unsatisfactorily modelled (bureaucrats). Fourth, the emphasis on the re-election constraint would seem to be too great; in reality, for example, politicians resign, cabinets fall, parties sometimes do not want to share government responsibility, politicians sometimes have career ambitions in the private sector. Moreover, in multi-party systems with coalition governments, it is unclear how this constraint should be modelled. Fifth, and in my view most important, the in the Downs' tradition truely innovative aspect of the model - the emphasis on ideology - misses a theoretical elaboration and operationalization in terms of individual interests or preferences; there is even no attempt to relate ideology, to the arguments in the popularity function, which is particularly unsatisfactory from the adhered viewpoint of methodological individualism. Notwithstanding this critique, the Frey and Schneider model has definitely been a step forward in the development of political economic models. Particularly, because of the attention given to institutional aspects. In this respect their model compares favourably with some other more general political economic models that have been developed recently, such as the median voter model of Meltzer and Richard (1981, 1983) and the interesting but highly abstract game-theoretical model of Aumann and Kurz (1978).

1.3. Critique

The purpose of the previous section was to give an impression of the enormous amount of work that has been carried out in the field of (positive) modern political economy after its definitive start in the late fifties. Many tools have been developed, with applications to a wide variety of subjects. Given the space constraint it was unavoidable to select, and subjective preferences will certainly have played a role here. Nevertheless, it is hoped that a fairly balanced bird's-eye view has been presented.

Before embarking upon an endeavour to bring the development of this research area into some perspective, I will first indicate a number of limitations and shortcomings of the present state of the art.

1. Why individuals at all vote in large scale elections, notwithstanding their negligible direct influence on the election outcome, has as yet not

been explained in a satisfactory way. This point will be returned to below.

2.   Regarding the behaviour of political parties, up till now relatively little attention has been paid to multi-party systems - which is no doubt partly due to the dominant Anglo-Saxon research orientation - as well as to the behaviour and influence of factions within political parties. As most democracies are characterized by multi-party systems and most parties, if not all of them, qualify as heterogeneous collectivities, much more research effort should be put in the study of such issues as the formation and the behaviour of coalition governments, and the impact of the party-line (party discipline) on the behaviour of politicians (and bureaucrats).
Another neglected area concerning the dynamics of party behaviour is the formation, the development and possibly demise of political parties.

3.   In relation to the previous point, it should further be noted that the existing models of coalition formation are not at all related to models of voting behaviour, in spite of the fact that parties are made up by voters (an exception is van Winden, 1984).

4.   As regards political systems, moreover, attention has almost exclusively been directed towards democracies with regular elections, in spite of the fact that they form a minority (an exception is Lafay, 1981).

5.   Too much attention is paid to elections as a medium to influence government behaviour; particularly in the so-called political economic models. There are many other instruments of political participation, however, which may not only be used between elections but also during election campaigns to influence its outcome; think of campaign contributions, lobbies, pressure group activity (cf. Breton, 1974, and Foley, 1978).

6. Due to the neglect of institutions and the narrow view of political influence, spatial models of electoral competition have difficulties with the explanation of the degree of political stability that is observed in reality (cf. Shepsle, 1979).

7. Relationships between governmental bodies within a country - between central and local governments - or of different countries have as yet been hardly investigated in a more systematic way. As regards the latter, it can, more generally, be said that issues of international political economy have received relatively little attention up till now in political economic models (cfr. Frey, 1984; Holler, 1987).

8. Very few general political economic models - that is, macro-economic models with endogenous government behaviour - have been developed so far. Empirical application of these models is often hampered by a lack of adequate data. The existing models are deficient with respect to the integration of the behaviour of, in particular, bureaucrats and pressure groups.

9. The maintained hypothesis regarding the behaviour of politicians and bureaucrats are too simplistic and at any rate highly unsatisfactory from the adhered point of view of methodological individualism, as the relationship between the assumed goals - be it vote maximization, ideology operationalized as a target share of government expenditure in national income, or budget maximization - and something that could be recognized as the self-interest of individuals is not made explicit. In this context it is, inter alia, important that the relationship between politicians and political parties is sufficiently elaborated and that also sufficient account is taken of the internal organization structure of the government sector. A similar critique holds for the popularity functions used to describe voting behaviour. It is not made clear why voters would at all be interested in the level or the development of the macro-economic variables employed in these functions. Why would a self-interested pensioner for example care for the unemployment rate?

(cf. Hibbs, 1982). Remarkably, moreover, is the neglect of the consumption of government goods in these models (cf. Schram and van Winden, 1987).

10. "Pocketbook politics, in the guise of economic self-interest, narrowly defined, figures heavily - and rather uncritically - in social science thinking about politics" (Kinder and Kiewiet, 1981, p. 131). As noted earlier, empirical results regarding voting behaviour - as well as theoretical reflections (think of the general lack of political influence of a single individual) - do not seem to support a narrow interpretation of self interest. It is increasingly felt that the relevant level of analysis would be that of social groups, instead of the purely individual (pocketbook) or, for that matter, national (sociotropic) level (cf. Kramer, 1983; Weatherford, 1983). Not only do people seem to refer to such groups for information about what may happen to themselves - mediated by opinion leaders -, it is also the level from which social norms originate. Thus, a better starting point may thereby also be obtained for a more systematic study of the importance of social norms, which are either totally neglected in the literature or introduced in some ad hoc fashion (such as 'civic duty' in order to explain voter turnout).

Furthermore, it should be mentioned here that a shift in focus from the purely individual level to that of social groups will strain the maintained hypothesis of given preferences. As people's reference groups may change over time, by their own initiative or due to government policies (cf. the promotion of stock-ownership - "people's capitalism"), their preferences may as well.

1.4. Perspective

Many of the limitations and shortcomings enumerated in the previous section are of the normal "further research is needed" or "subject of ongoing research" nature. Given the youth of this field of research it is not surprisingly that it is still strongly characterized by first-approaches' awaiting further development. This is not to say that there are no obstacles in the way here. In this final section I would like to shortly indicate three - in my view - major hurdles that will have to be taken.

The first one has to do with the shift in focus from the purely individudal level to that of social groups that is advocated in the recent literature. Apart from the fact that, albeit not necessarily in principle, this shift will in practice entail a less strict interpretation of methodological individualism - which need as such not meet great resistance as we have seen that it is already loosely interpreted in many of the theoretical models that have been proposed - there is a more serious problem to be confronted here.As any theory demands abstraction, it will evoke the question, namely, which social groups one should particularly concentrate at. Now there are some venerable old strands of economic thought that are particularly suggestive in this context. I refer to the Marxian tradition which emphasizes the significance of the position that people have with respect to the structure of the production process for the distinction between politically relevant social groups. However, proponents of methodological individualism and of Marxian economic theory do not seem to be very fond of each other. The traceable ideological (political) element in the development of these two approaches is a serious problem in this respect, as it hampers a fresh appreciation of their potential. That some synthesis of these approaches may lead to useful and interesting results is suggested by the so-called interest function approach' (cf. van Winden, 1983, 1987; see also Van Velthoven, 1988). Taking as starting point that individuals on their own typically lack political influence and that, therefore, representative individuals of social groups become focal points for their behaviour, an elementary distinction is made between four such groups on the basis of their position in the production process (for reasons I cannot go into now), to wit: government sector workers; private sector workers; capital owners; and 'dependants', with an income out of transfers. For the representative individual of each group an 'elementary interest function' is formulated which represents the utility to that individual of the market and non-market goods that are at her/his disposal. An important feature of the approach is that it allows for the fact that more than one such function may be, or become, relevant for an individual's behaviour due to the following factors or motives; innate altruism, multiple positions (membership of different groups), mobility (a perceived probability of arriving at a different position), and pressure (the accumulation of which may leed to 'vested interests'). This leads to the formulation of 'complex interest functions', which are weighted representations of elementary interest functions, where the weights indicate the extent to which the interests of other groups are furthered as a result of the foregoing motives. Note that in case of pressure the interests of other groups are served because the individual is forced to do so, which distinguishes this motive from the others. Notice further that preferences will be subject to change, since motives generally change over time.

Although the behaviour of the government is assumed to be ultimately determined by the interests of those employed by that organization (the government sector workers; that is, politicians and bureaucrats), the interests of outside groups will be furthered to the extent that the afore mentioned motives are effective. It should be added here, that if government policies have incentive effects the interests of the groups for which these incentives are operating will (further) be taken into account in so far as this is considered by government sector workers to be conducive to the realization of their own interests (this factor is called 'structural coercion'). The interest function approach differs from the Marxian approach, inter alia, by the more prominent place given to individuals and the distinction between four social classes. Moreover, the desirability of formalization (quantitative theory) is emphasized. With respect to the traditional public choice approach it particularly distinguishes itself through its focus on social groups in relation to the social production structure - instead of a rigid methodological individualism - and its emphasis on forms of structural coercion and pressure other than those related to elections only. The approach has been applied - theoretically as well as empirically - to a number of topics, such as taxation, social security, government budget deficits, local government behaviour under fiscal federalism, politically induced economic fluctuations (business cycles as well as long waves), voting behaviour and government coalition formation (see van Winden, 1987, for references). The results obtained so far not only strongly suggest that further elaboration of this approach may be worthwhile but more generally that a shift in focus from the purely individual level to that of social groups is feasible and rewarding.

A second major hurdle that my hinder the further development of political economics (including the interest function approach) concerns the modelling of bargaining processes or pressure activity in a wide sense. Although an almost omnipresent problem - within the political sphere as well as in the interaction between the government sector and the private sector - it has not yet been satisfactorily solved, or even squarely faced, in most areas. Recent developments in game theory, especially the so-called non-cooperative approach to cooperative outcomes, seem to be encouraging in this respect but without much impact yet on political economic modelling.

A third major hurdle, finally, concerns the lack of adequate data to apply and test political economic theories. Partly this is no doubt again a matter of time, and an inconvenience that all researchers have to live with. However, it is not to be neglected that in this case the information has largely to be delivered by the very organization that is to be studied and possibly criticized for its behaviour, while, moreover, it cannot be forced to do so by another organization in the same way as private organizations are by the government. The statement in a recent publicaton of the Dutch Central Bureau of Statistics (CBS, 1983, p. 61) that statistics related to the government sector itself have never been among the most systematic, best defined and best classified parts of the official statistics gives food for thoughts in this respect. Apart from this, the informational problem regarding the way that perceptions and expectations are formed should perhaps be mentioned. However, this problem is not very peculiar to the subject matter of modern political economy but pervades the whole body of economic theory.

Notwithstanding the hurdles that political economics will have to take for its further development, its strength is already such that its place within the economics discipline - as well as political science, for that matter - seems secured. It derives this strength in particular from the following achievements. First, in trying to remedy a serious deficiency of mainstream economics - the neglect of political decision-making as an important allocation mechanism for scarce resources - it has shown it to be possible to go beyond vague assertions and to develop useful models that can (in principle) be applied and tested against rival hypotheses. Second, it has opened up the possibility of integrated political economic models that allow for the endogenous character of political decision-making. This is also important for the modelling of private sector behaviour - as endeavoured in traditional macro-economic models - in so far as this behaviour is co-determined by anticipated government policies (cf. Lucas, 1976). It follows that so-called scenarios regarding government policies are based on misspecified models to the extent that private sector behaviour is indeed influenced that way. Third, it has led to a rethinking of the theory of economic policy. If the state can no longer be considered as the exogenous, benevolent dictator which (implicitly) figured in the traditional theory of economic policy, the effectiveness of policy advices will, consequently, also have to be judged from a different angle. This change in vision will most probably entail a shift of attention away from the state towards other agents involved in the political decision-making process. It is, furthermore, to be expected that it will lead to a greater attention for the structural aspects of that process (the 'rules of the game'), their impact as well as their susceptibility to reform. It is here that two other lines of political economic thinking - neglected so far because of our focus on positive theories - becomes of potential interest, to wit: constitutional economics (cf. Brennan and Buchanan, 1980; McKenzie, 1984) and social choice (concerned with the analysis of systems of choice where the primitives are preferences and rules;

cf. Schofield, 1985, or Suzumura, 1983). It is, finally, regarded as a strength of modern political economy that it shows the possibility of the unificaton of the social sciences - in at least one area of interest, and the fruitfulness of the application of the tools and methods of economic theory in this respect. It has thereby opened up the possibility of rigorous quantitative theory development and, through its preference for formalization, the testing of these theories against either real-life data or data generated in a laboratory setting (experiments, computer simulations).

The research programme of political economics is ambitious. It has also met resistance from within the economics profession as well as from other professions. A partly cynical explanation for this resistance is offered by Stigler (1984, pp. 311-312); "one reason for this scientific conservatism (...) is presumably that older scholars wish to protect their specific human capital (...). Schumpeter's view that a science progresses through the dying off of its old professors has some truth. A second reason for the conservatism is that these extentions of economics have not in general assisted economics in dealing with their traditional economic problems (...). I believe that, in time, there will be a useful feedback (...)." However, this may be, there can be no doubt in my view about the relevance of the questions that modern political economy poses and tries to answer.

References

Aumann, R.J. and Kurz (1987), Power and taxes in a multi-commodity economy (updated), Journal of Public Economics, 9, pp. 139-161.

Axelrod, R. (1970), Conflict of interest, Markham, Chicago.

Becker, G.C. (1983), A theory of competition among pressure groups for political influence, Quarterly Journal of Economics, 9, pp. 371-400.

Bergstrom, T.C. and R.P. Goodman (1973), Private demands for public goods, American Economic Review, 63, pp. 280-296.

38

Borooah, V K. and F. van der Ploeg (1983), Political aspects of the economy, C.U.P., Cambridge.

Brennan, G. and J.M. Buchanan (1980), The power to tax: analytical foundations of a fiscal constitution, C.U.P., Cambridge.

Breton, A. (1974), The economic theory of representative government, Aldine, Chicago.

Breton, A. and R. Wintrobe (1982), The logic of bureaucratic conduct, C.U.P., Cambridge.

CBS (1983), CBS-select 2,, Staatsuitgeverij, 's-Gravenhage.

Coleman, J.S. (1971), Internal processes governing party positions in elections, Public Choice, 2, pp. 35-69.

Coughlin, P., and S. Nitzan (1981), Electoral outcomes with probabilistic voting and Nash social welfare maxima, Journal of Public Economics, 15, pp. 113-121.

De Swaan, A. (1973), Coalition theories and cabinet formations, Elsevier, Amsterdam.

Downs, A. (1957), An economic theory of democracy, Harper and Row, New York.

Enelow, J.M., and M.J. Hinich (1984), The spatial theory of voting, C.U.P., Cambridge

Esty, D.C., and R.E. Caves (1983), Market structure and political influence: new data on political expenditures, activity, and success, Economic Inquiry, 21,pp. 24-38.

Foley, D.K. (1987), State expenditure from a Marxist perspective, Journal of Public Economics, 9, pp. 221-238.

Frey, B.S. (1978a), Modern political economy, Wiley, New York.

Frey, B.S. (1978b), Politico-economic models and cycles, Journal of Public Economics, 9, pp. 203-220.

Frey, B.S. (1984), International political economics,Basil Blackwell, Oxford.

Frey, B.S. and L.J. Lau (1968), Towards a mathematical model of government behaviour, Zeitschrift für Nationalökonomie, 28, pp; 355-380.

Friedman, L.S. (1984), Microeconomic policy analysis, McGraw-Hill, New York.

Gärtner, M. (1981), A politicoeconomic model of wage inflation, De

Economist, 129, pp. 183-205.

Hibbs, D.A., Jr. (1982), The dynamics of political support for American presidents among occupational and partisan groups, American Journal of Political Science, 26, pp.312-332.

Hibbs, D.A., Jr., and H. Fassbender (1981), Contemporary political economy, North-Holland, Amsterdam.

Holler, M.J. (1987),The logic of multiparty systems, Kluwer, Dordrecht.

Jaarsma, B., A. Schram and F.A.A.M. van Winden (1986), On the voting participation of public bureaucrats, Public Choice, 48, pp. 183-187.

Kinder, D.R., and D.R. Kiewiet (1981), Sociotropic politics: the American Case, British Journal of Political Science, 11, pp. 129-161.

Kramer, G.H. (1983), The ecological fallacy revisited: aggregate-versus individual-level findings on economics and elections and sociotropic voting, American Political Science Review, 77, pp. 92-111.

Lafay, J.K. (1981), Empirical analysis of politico-economic interaction in the East European Countries, Soviet Studies.

Layer, M. (1985), The relationship between coalition policy and party policy, European Journal of Political Economy, 1/2, pp. 243-169.

Lucas, R.E., Jr. (1976), Econometric policy evaluation, a critique, Journal of Monetary Economics, supplement series, 1, pp. 19-46.

McKenzie, R.B. (1984), Constitutional economics, Lexington Books, Lexington.

Meltzer, A.H., and S.F. Richard (1981), A rational theory of the size of government, Journal of Political Economy, 89, pp. 914-927.

Meltzer, A.H., and S.F. Richard (1983), Test of a rational theory of the size of government, Public Choice, 41, pp. 403-418.

Migué, J.L., and G. Bélanger (1974), Toward a general theory of managerial discretion, Public Choice, 17, pp. 27-43.

Mueller, D.C. (1979), Public Choice, C.U.P., Cambridge.

Mueller, D.C. (1987), The growth of government, IMF-Staff Papers, pp. 115-149.

Mueller, D.C., and P. Murrell (1986), Interest groups and the size of government, Public Choice, 48, pp. 125-145.

Murrell, P. (1984), An examination of the factors affecting the formation of interest groups in OECD countries, Pubic Choice, 43, pp. 151-171.

Niskanen, W.A. (1974), Bureaucracy and representative government, Aldine, Chicago.

Nordhaus, W.D. (1975), The political business cycle, Review of economic studies, 42, pp. 169-190.

Olson, M. (1965), The logic of collective action, Harvard University Press, Cambridge (Mass).

Orzechowski, W. (1977), Econopmic models of bureaucracy: survey, extensions, and evidence, in : T.E. Borcherding (ed.), Budgets and bureaucrats: the sources of government growth, Duke University Press, Durham, pp. 229-259.

Paldam, M. (1981), A preliminary survey of the theories and findings of vote and popularity functions, European Journal of Political Research, 9, pp. 181-199.

Plotnick, R.D. (1986), An interest group model of direct income redistribution, Review of Economics and Statistics, pp. 594-602.

Pommerehne, W.W. (1978), Institutional approaches to public expenditure, Journal of Public Economics, 9, pp. 255-280.

Renaud, P.S.A., and F.A.A.M. van Winden (1987), On the importance of elections and ideology for government policy in a multi-party system, in : Holler 'The logic of multiparty systems'; Kluwer, Dordrecht, pp. 191-207.

Riker, W.H. (1962), The theory of political coalitions, Yale University Press, New Haven

Romer, T. and H. Rosenthal (1979), The elusive median voter, Journal of Public Economics, 12, pp. 143-170.

Salamon, L.M., and J.J. Siegfried (1977), Economic power and political influence: the impact of industry structure on public policy, American Political Science Review, 71, pp. 1026-1043.

Schofield, N.J. (1985), Social choice and democracy, Springer-Verlag, Berlin.

Schofield, N.J., and M. Laver (1987), Bargaining theory and cabinet stability in European governments, in : Holland (see above), pp. 137-152.

Schram, A.J.H.C., and F.A.A.M. van Winden (1987), Modelling voter behaviour in a multi-party system, paper presented at the 1987 EPCS meeting at Reggio Calabria and the 1987 ESEM in Copenhagen, University of Amsterdam.

Schumpeter, J.A. (1947), Institutional arrangements and equilibrium in multidimensional voting models, American Journal of Political Science, 23, pp. 27-39.

Stigler, G.J. (1972), Economic competition and political competition, Public Choice, 12, pp. 91-106.

Stigler, G.J. (1984), Economics - the imperial science?, Scandinavian Journal of Economics, 86, pp. 301-313.

Suzumura, K. (1983), Rational choice, collective decisions, and social welfare, C.U.P., Cambridge.

Taylor, M., and M. Laver (1973), Government coalitions in Western-Europe, European Journal of Political Research, 1, pp. 2205-248.

Tollison, R.D. (1982), Rent seeking: a survey, Kyklos, 35, pp. 575-602.

Van den Doel, H. (1979), Democracy and welfare economics, C.U.P., Cambridge

Van Velthoven, B.C.J. (1988), The endogenization of government behaviour in macroeconomic models, Leyden University.

van Winden, F.A.A.M. (1983), On the interaction between state and private sector, a study in political economics, North-Holland, Amsterdam.

van Winden, F.A.A.M. (1984), Towards a dynamic theory of cabinet formation, in: M.J. Holler (ed.), Coalitions and collective action, Physica-Verlag, Würzburg, 11, pp. 145-159.

van Winden, F.A.A.M. (1987), Man in the public sector, De Economist, 135, pp. 1-28.

Weatherford, M.S. (1978), Economic conditions and electoral outcomes: class differences in the political response to recession, American Journal of Political Science, 22, pp. 917-938.

Weber, M. (1972 (1922)), Wirtschaft und Gesellschaft, fünfte revidierte Auflage, Mohr, Tübingen.

Wittman, D.A. (1973), Parties as utility maximizers, American Political Science Review, 67, pp. 490-498.

Wittman, D.A. (1987), Elections with n voters, m candidates and k issues, in: Holler (see above), pp. 129-134.

2 CRITICAL NOTES ON THE NEOCLASSICAL THEORY OF THE INTERACTION OF POLITICS AND ECONOMICS.
A comment on van Winden

Jörg Glombowski

2.1. Introduction

Economists find it increasingly attractive to deal with political behaviour and politico-economic interaction. Those active in this relatively new line of research seem to be convinced that their work is fruitful, although they are prepared to concede that there is much work left to do. This confidence seems to stem from the assessment that the same methodological principles, which have been so successfully applied in economic theory proper, can equally well be used in the neighbouring disciplines of political science and sociology (1). By this I refer to methodological individualism, which holds individual actions to be the adequate starting point of analysis and rational choices to explain those actions.

As I have serious doubts about the alleged successes of neoclassical economics, I am sceptical with regard to the fruitfulness of its expeditions into new territorries (2). The critical remarks I will put forward, must be discounted, however, for two reasons. First of all, I am not a specialist in the field and do not command the extensive knowledge of the relevant literature as van Winden or Borooah do. Secondly, I must confess that I have experimented with politico-economic models myself that do not differ so much from those I am going to criticize.

Julien van den Broeck (ed.), Public Choice, 43-57.
© *1988 by Kluwer Academic Publishers and Association of Post-Keynesian Studies.*

2.2. Biases in emphasis

Instead of putting forward a series of abstract methodological arguments let me start from questions that I feel are relevant but which are (rather) neglected in the economic theory of politics. Its emphasis lies on capitalist democracies (3), in which (a) choices of voters matter in the framework of party competition, (b) those choices are derived from preferences vis-a-vis economic conditions and (c) the results of elections have a decisive impact on government formation and economic policies.

There are a lot of capitalist countries in the world, to which this framework does not apply and I just mention Chile, Taiwan and Kenya as examples. These examples cannot simple be dismissed as exeptions to the rule. While one-party regimes clearly dominate in Africa and military dictatorships have been frequent in recent Latin American history, it is not easy to find working examples for (Western) democracies in Asia either. Yet one might expect that there exist links between the economic and the political subsystems in those countries as well, which, consequently, would have to be explained. One might argue that productive political economists are not concentrated in those countries and that their unfamiliarity with the prevailing situations could explain the bias in question. But I think it is also due to the approaches used. While they claim to be general, they actually are rather limited in scope (4). Furthermore, one might argue that the object of modern political economics is the developed capitalist countries only. Such an answer would not be entirely satisfactory either, as there are sufficient examples of nondemocratic rule in twentieth century Europe. While conventional political science did address these cases, the contributions of the economic theory of politics have still to be delivered (5).

The United States, the United Kingdom and the Netherlands figure among the select group of rather old and stable democracies. Most of the present-day democratic institutions are considerably younger (including those capitalist core countries of Japan, Italy and (West) Germany). For all of them the general suffrage of adult males, let alone of all adults is a rather recent achievement, if considered in historical perspective (6). One would wish a theory of politics, whether "economic" or not, to explain why and under which circumstances its object(s) came into being, yet I do not know of any "economic" counterparts to "political" analyses as exemplified by that of Therborn.

Another aspect of the same problematic is the question whether, why and under which circumstances the "marriage" of capitalism and democracy tends to form the natural mode of functioning of a capitalist society. These are subjects which have been intensively discussed among left-wing political scientists (cf. e.g. Jessop 1978), but according to my knowledge contributions from modern political economics are missing. Do they take the correspondence of capitalism and democracy for granted as for instance Hayek would?

This criticism extends to the respective futures of capitalism and democracy. In the nineteenth century the belief was rather generally held that universal suffrage would lead to serious disruptions of the economic order as the poor would use their voting rights to "rob" the rich (7). Marxists shared this view in a special sense. In an exceptionally clear statement, Engels described the percentage of left votes only as an indicator of the organisational and ideological maturity of the proletariat to put a political end to an economic system which, according to Marx's theory, was doomed anyhow (see Engels 1969, p. 68). It is obvious that things have not worked out like this, but it still seems relevant to think about the future stability of the capitalist-democratic "marriage". Schumpeter, being one of the fathers of the idea of the political marketplace, in which voters choose among the political products offered by parties, paid due attention to this question as did Keynes, trying to devise ways for healthy survival. A major new analysis from a Radical standpoint has been recently provided by Bowles and Gintis (1986). By comparison, modern political economists seem to have narrowed their perspective.

2.3. Motivations of Politicians

Methodological individualism seems to be very precise when it comes to motivations, but I think this claim is not warranted. Some sketchy remarks on voters' and bureaucrats' motivations will be made later on. Here we will take only a quick look on the alleged motivations of politicians. According to van Winden's summary, the "basic assumption is that politicians - elected representatives - are motivated by their self-interest which is seen to be the income, power and prestige derived from being in office". These three motivations do not amount to the same. As every individual politician could be motivated by a very personal mixture of these components, a wide variety of behaviour is allowed and almost nothing excluded. While income could be defined reasonable in conventional terms, power is one of the most disputed concepts in political science and sociology, giving rise to numerous definitions and less operationalisations. As we define it loosely to be the capability to make others behave as one wants them to, the immediate question rises, what it is that the others should do: work hard, fight a war, vote in one's favour or what else? I guess "prestige" is an equally ambiguous term.

Even if one is prepared to accept the motivations mentioned they do not seem specific for politicians. One could equally well become a captain of industry, a famous lawyer or a general to pursue them. Although choices are crucial in methodological individualistic thought, it is neither explained why certain people choose to become politicians nor how they choose a party (if any). Some of the most interesting questions seem already to have been answered before the analysis starts (8).

Van Winden is also critical with respect to the translation of self-interest of individual politicians into vote maximization by parties, which is frequently assumed (his point 9). I share this view and would add that things do not become easier for methodological individualists if parties are assumed to follow ideological goals subject to reelection restrictions (Frey 1978). I do not mean to say this step is wrong - on the contrary. But for methodological individualists it puts the difficult task of explaining the ways in which social structures shape individual preferences which include views on social reality and desirable courses of action. In proposing the use of group-related interest functions, van Winden shortcuts these problems and rejects the individualistic dogma. I sympathize with his approach, but I am afraid the microfundamentalists of all countries will unite against the sin of "ad hoc-theorizing".

2.4. Institutional Variety

Between the bunch of national capitalist democracies there are enormous differences, which give rise to the general institutionalist question, whether a general theory can adequately cover this variety of appearances (9). In his critical remarks, van Winden explicitly emphasizes this institutional variety, but he seems to think that a certain redirection and intensification of research efforts could cope with the problem, i.e. would not necessitate us to abandon the vision of a unified theory of economics and politics. Let us consider some of the differences in order to assess their significance.

Obviously there is a lot of variety on the "supply side", i.e. the numbers as well as the characters of the competing parties. Moreover, there is a large variety of rules by which the numbers of votes are transformed into numbers of parliamentary representatives (election modalities) and numbers of representatives into members of government coalition formation). Models with only two competing parties derive their attractiveness from the fact that they help to avoid a lot of theoretical trouble in dealing with these complications. They even allow us to abstract from the genuine problem of qualitative differences between the "products" offered. In Nordhaus' model of the political business cycle Nordhaus 1975), interpreted as a parliamentary cycle, the oppositioin would precisely do what the majority party does if it had the chance to do so, i.e. if it were ruling instead. Thus you may call them "A" or "B" just as you would label duapolists offering a homogeneous product. Of course, that is not what politics is about and it seems much

more reasonable to place the competitors on a right-left coordinate (10)
If you turn to three or more parties you need more coordinates with
different qualitative significance along which to define the stance of
parties. But while you can possibly identify left and right in all cases
other axes may be more nation-specific. Taking Belgium as an example
one could define a religious axis, a language cleavage and an
environmental coordinate. Methodological individualists would have a hard
time to interpret this particular supply structure and voting behaviour in
terms of self-interest only (11). Additional coordinates would be different
for other nations, featuring e.g. sexual, racial, regional or generational
differences. The existence of voters' preferences with regard to those
dimensions must be assumed and the states of society to which voters
react should be represented in terms of variables related to these
dimensions. By doing so, however, the national models might become
very different and a lot of them would possibly show a very restricted
relevance of economic orientations.

Moreover, the problem of dynamic change comes up again. We
should be prepared to explain why the number of parties changes, why
former existing parties disappear or change their characters and why new
parties can establish themselves amidst the settled ones. To do so we
would need a dynamic theory of preferences and of the rules of the
game. While I do not see how the first requirement can be achieved
the second one would have to be based on principles analogous to those
found in Neo-Schumpeterian and Radical economics (12). The parties
would have to be taken as advancing their goals not only by playing
according to the rules but also by trying to changes the rules in
directions advantageous to their respective causes. This involves a whole
range of moves which are well-known from political practice: banning
parties, regulating party financing, changing press laws, raising or
lowering election thresholds, changing the boundaries of districts, limiting
the possibility of re-election etc. Besides changes of formal legislation
there is a whole series of 'unfair' practices" available of which the
multiple misuses of executive power are a subcategory (13).

2.5. Restrictions on the Exercise of Political Power

The ideal picture of parliamentary democracy shows how voters decide directly about its representatives and indirectly about the nature of the government and the policies pursued. Thus political power would indirectly be exercised by the people. Of course, nobody believes this picture to give a true account of the fact, but the objections made are very different and depend on theoretical as well as political perspectives.

Public choice theorists point to the disturbing impacts of the bureaucrats' and the politicians' self-interest as well as to the deviations caused by pressure groups. Marxists traditionally have stressed the limited role of parliaments by describing the state as an agency of capital which has to fulfill certain necessary functions, i.e. promoting capital accumulation and securing the legitimation of the system (14). According to van Winden the economic theory of politics puts too much emphasis on elections and too little on pressure groups and other forms of representation when it comes to explain the determinants of political action.

I think it cannot be denied that parties make a difference (15), which implies that elections matter. The crucial task seems to me to determine the exact measure of significance, which in view of what has been said above, could vary substantially between countries as well as in time. I think that the notions of power and restrictions are crucial for such an analysis.

Let us take the power of a single majority party as a starting point. Public choice theorists are inclined to assume that such a party possesses all the power while the opposotion is virtually powerless. This view certainly has to be modified considerably. Most obviously it does not hold if there is a catalogue of issues for which the constitution demands qualified majorities to take decisions upon. Secondly, there may be other parliamentary bodies whether elected or not (e.g. a second house of parliament; state, regional and local parliaments) in which the "majority party" forms a minority and therefore has to search for compromises whenever those bodies share in the decision rights (16).

Thirdly, we will mostly have a constitutionally division of powers (trias politica) which limits the measure of legislative power.

One could argue that these arguments are merely formal as the government would consist of members of the majority party which also would control bureaucratic and other important appointments (e.g. to the directory of the cental bank or the high level courts). Yet they will generally have to deal with people appointed by former governments or parliaments with a different composition and who still have (considerable) laps of time to go (17).

It is obvious that we add to those limitations if we take coalition governments or the existence of fractions within a single majority party into account (18). Moreover, things become more complicated in case of mixed presidential-parliamentary regimes.

Quite another dimension is opened up where political power proper is brought into relation with social or economic power. Political parties use to have specific patterns of support in society and often are linked to non-political organisations. We only have to consider phenomena of "denominational segregation" ("verzuiling") or "labour movement" to indicate this dimension. For political parties this opens up the possibility to enforce their political position by cooperating with social movements or economically powerful groups. This applies for the opposition as well as for the ruling party or parties. It shows once again that an opposition party must not at all be powerless even if its position in parliament is weak. Its outside allies could support it for example by strikes, demonstrations, boycotts, advertising campaigns etc. Of course, the opportunities are not strictly symmetrical, because ruling parties have more possibilities to actively creating support by changing rules (e.g. trade union laws), rechanneling government spending towards congenial activities (e.g. certain types of education, research programmes, economic sectors, etc.), influencing public media (19) or by deliberately creating economic dependency of certain social groups from party controlled public authorities (20). Those links between political parties and social collectivities also work the other way around. The support of parties may have its price in terms of favourable policies (clientelism).

While the economic theory of politics pays some attention to the limitations of power of elected representatives by bureaucracies and pressure groups, it does not seem to attach appropriate weight to the multiple forms of non-elective interactions of the political and the other players in the game.

Last but not least, we should mention in this context all those limitations of political action which cannot be related to strategic adversary behaviour of people or organized groups, but to given circumstances or trends. A simple example would be world market dynamics, including the internationalizatoin of production, changing direction of capital flows and exchange rate fluctuations. Marxists have tended to stress either the strong influence of economically powerful groups ("monopoly capital") on politics or - alterenatively - to narrow down the choice set of political action to almost zero. Both devices turn out to produce the same type of results, i.e. the capitalist state will practise "capitalist" policies, irrespective of whether for instance social-democratic or conservative parties gain political majorities. But if parties and the specific brand of the democratic game peoples play do not matter much, you are entitled to abstract from them on a high level of theorizing (21). It should be clear that I do not subscribe to such abortive views on the character of politico-economic interactions. Yet I feel that the economic theory of politics underestimates restrictions for and influences on politics from outside its own domain.

2.6. What are Political Issues ?

In politico-economic models the most common assumptions about voting behaviour seem to be:

   a)   that voters maximize their individual utilities;
   b)   that preferences are defined with regard to economic circumstances only;
   c)   that the economic circumstances are described by standard macroeconomic variables;

d)   that preferences are stable over time;

e)   that voters do not influence the choice set, i.e. number and character of the competing parties.

Van Winden has already made critical remarks with regard to some of these points, especially (a), (c) and (e). I would like to add some. First of all it seems to me that economists should be very careful in assuming that people are mainly concerned with what they themselves feel essential, i.e. economics. Even if it cannot be denied that economic performance and future programmes may play a relevant role in voters' decisions, it is not apriori obvious to which degree they do. It has been argued for instance that U.S. voters are more concerned about economics than European (Hibbs) and that the importance of economic issues increases in time (Rose), but is also seems to be true that questions of war and peace remain crucial (22).

Also, it is not always certain in which way economic changes or performances would affect (groups of) voters. "Facts" are open to interpretation, "performances" may be attributed to different causes and measured against different expectations, while the interested parties will do their best to "assist" the voters in making up their minds (23).

Of course, all models have to assume, at least implicitly, differences between individual utility functions, otherwise everyone would vote for the same party. But it seems rather unsatisfactory to restrict oneself to the assumption of certain time-invariant statistical distribution functions, as this excludes group dynamics, social and individual learning processes and attempts to change ideological standpoints in one's favour. The latter attempts culminate in election campaigns, which also put certain major issues to the fore which are often qualitative in kind and historically unique, e.g. whether or not to enter the Common Market, to change union legislation, to nationalize industries, to establish major nuclear power stations etc. We have to face the possibility that elections change in significance according to what is at stake. For instance they could mark definite historical turning points. To put it in the words of Bowles and Gintis, who identify exceptional elections in the

U.S.A. at the lower turning points of two former long waves:

"... old alignments may change, and new electoral coalitions emerge, sometimes reforming the dominant party from within, sometimes establishing a new dominant party. Electoral realignments took place at the height of the last two crisis periods, around what the political scientists call the critical election years, 1896 and 1934-1936." (Bowles/Gintis 1985, p. 96-97).

Although I agree with most of the critical points van Winden made, I differ somewhat with respect to the conclusions. While he expects significant progress from extended use of mathematical and statistical modelling techniques familiar to modern economists, I am more sceptical. Where he is looking forward to a unification of the social sciences along the lines suggested by economics, I would attach more weight to develop the old-fashioned interdisciplinary contacts. Differences in assessments often can be traced back to differences in questions. I am afraid that the economic theory of politics can only deliver limited contributions to the questions I find the most important in political theory.

Notes

(1)   An early example for the far reaching claims with respect to political science is Black 1950. For the case of sociology see Franz 1986.

(2)   As neoclassical economics has been accused of "imperialism", I should perhaps better talk of the new "colonies" instead.

(3)   I am referring to the theoretical perspective here. Of course, when it comes to empirical applications, certain specific aspects of the chosen object(s), e.g. a specific country, have to be (and are) taken into account to some degree.

(4)   There is, of course, a parallel to this in economics. While the neoclassical approach claimed generality, it did not prove strong enough to prevent the development of the economics of underdevelopment.

(5)   This judgement may be due to insufficient knowledge of the

literature on my part.

(6) For detailed historical informtion on this see Therborn 1977. With regard to the USA he comments: "The Fifteenth Amendmend enfranchised the blacks in the northern states, but it took another hundred years for it to take effect in the South... The Amendmend had been passed shortly before the centenary of the republic, but is was only just in time for the bicentennial celebrations that the United States fully qualified as a bourgeois democracy.' (p. 17) Cf. also Bowles/Edwards 1985, p. 379 on this point.

(7) This explains, why in most countries voting rights were only granted stepwise, starting with taxpayers or landowners or head of families only, i.e. very small percentages of the population.

(8) A similar problem occurs in neoclassical general equilibrium economics. Why do agents in the face of a perfect credit market decide to sell their labour power to others instead of hiring the labour of others? This problem is addressed by the rational choice Marxist John Roemer (1986 , p. 88)

(9) For a recent critical comment on political business cycle theory from an institutionalist perspective see May 1987.

(10) One could argue that at least for the United States that would not make much sense because there are no identifiable party lines and the Democrats and Republicans are both right-wing parties. I do not feel competent to judge but I think this would be an exaggeration suggested by an European perspective.

(11) De Clercq and Naert (1985) do not seem to realize that their methodological individualist position (cf. p. IX) is at odds with their (informative) description of Belgian politics (chapter 7).

(12) Bowles and Edwards characterize the Radical perspective on competition as follows: "In der radikalen Ökonomie maximieren die Unternehmer ebenfalls die Profite, aber sie tun das vornehmlich dadurch, dass sie gerade jene Parameter zu ändern versuchen, die im neoklassischen Modell exogen behandelt werden: Die Präferenzen, die staatliche Politik, die Techniken und die Art des Wettbewerbs." (Bowles/Edwards 1986, p. 9).

\

(13) The famous film "Z" by Costas-Gravas provides a good illustration of the rich spectrum of means.

(14) The irrelevance of voting decisions is postulated by Sutcliffe when he observes with respect to post war Europe: "Seldom had people been asked to vote so often and seldom had it seemed to make less difference." (Sutcliffe 1983, p. 34).

(15) See Hibbs (1977)-, Rose (1980) and Rothschild (1986).

(16) The Federal Republic of Germany is a very good case for illustration. The states (Länder) have their own parliaments with exclusive rights in the area of cultural and educational affairs and competing legislative rights in a number of other fields. Here the majorities may differ from that in the central parliament, the Bundestag. Moreover, the second chamber, the Bundesrat, which consists of the representatives of state governments, has a relevant impact on the central legislation, while it may have a majority differing from that of the Bundestag.

(17) One can try to incorporate this kind of limitation into politico-economic models by emphasizing the role of initial conditions and by introducing a certain inertia (cf. Frey 1978), but things may be "worse" than that. To take another German example: How can you effectively sentence Nazi criminals when the large majority of judges have been appointed by them and their "qualifications" for the assigned jobs have not changed much?

(18) The Japanese Liberal Democratic Party is a particular good example for the latter type of restriction.

(19) This seems to happen most notoriously in France.

(20) A good example for the latter has been the creation of peasants' cooperatives by the Japanese state on which the peasants depended heavily in the face of foreign trade and domestic market regulations (see Pempel/Tsunekawa 1979).

(21) Of course, these approaches create specific puzzles, only to be "solved" by specific rhetorics.

(22) The Falkland-war is only one example in an unpleasantly long series of relevant conflicts.

(23) The same development of variables could mean quite different things to people(s) at the same time or at different laps of time, e.g. a growtht rate of three per cent may be highly welcome now, while twice as much possibly caused disapppointment some twenty years ago. When the "Stabilitätsgesetz" was passed in West-Germany at the end of the sixties, providing the state with new legal instruments and obligations, a juridical commentator interpreted the task of providing price stability to mean that the state had to eliminate any inflation rate higher than one per cent!.

References

Black, D., Die Einheit von Politischer Wissenschaft und Wirtschaftswissenschaft, in : M. Shubik (ed.), Spieltheorie und Sozialwissenschaften, Hamburg (S. Fischer) 1965, pp. 119-128 (originally in Economic Journal 1950).

Bowles, S., Edwards, R., Understanding Capitalism. Competition, Command, and Change in the U.S. Economy, New York (Harper & Row), 1985.

Bowles, S., Edwards, R., Neuere theoretische Entwicklungen in der radikalen politischen Ökonomie, Merwert nr. 28, Dec. 1986, pp. 1-15.

Bowles, S., Gintis, H., Democracy and Capitalism. Property, Community, and the Contradictions of Modern Social Thought, New York (Basic Books) 1986.

De Clercq, M., Naert, F., De politieke markt, Kluwer 1985.

Engels, F., Der Ursprung der Familie, des Privateigentums und des Staats, in : Marx-Engels-Werke, vol. 21, Berlin (Dietz) 1969, pp. 25-173.

Frans, P., Der "Contrained Choice" - Ansatz als gemeinsamer Nenner individualistischer Ansätze in der Soziologie. Ein Vorschlag zur theoretischen Integration, in : Kölner Zeitschrift für Soziologie und Sozialpsychologie, 38/1986, pp. 32-54.

Frey, B.S., Politico-Economic Models and Cycles, Journal of Public Economics 9/1978, pp. 203-220.

Hibbs, D.A., Jr., Political Parties and Macroeconomic Policy, merican Political Science Review 71/1977, pp. 1467-1487.

Jessop, B., Capitalism and Democracy: the Best Possible Shell? in : ittlejohn, G. (ed.), Power and the State, London 1978, pp. 10-51.

May, A.M., The Political Business Cycle: An Institutional Critique nd Reconstruction, in : Journal of Economic Issues 21/1987, pp. 713-722.

Nordhaus, W.D., The Political Business Cycle, Review of Economic tudies 42/1975, pp. 169-190.

Pempel, T.J., Tsunekawa, K., Corporatism without Labour?, The apanese Anomaly, in : Schmitter, P.C., Lehmbruch, G. (eds.), rends towards Corporatist Intermediation, Beverly Hills / London 1979, p. 231-270.

Roemer, J., New Directions in the Marxian Theory of Class, in : oemer J. (ed.), Analytical Marxism, Cambridge/Paris (Cambridge niversity Press/Editions de la Maison des Sciences de l'Homme) 1986, p. 81-113.

Rose, R., Do Parties Make a Difference? Chatham, N.J. (Chatham ouse Publishers) 1980.

Rothschild, K.W., 'Left' and 'Right' in Central Europe, Kyklos 9/1986, pp. 359-76.

Sutcliffe, B., Hard Times, The World Economy in Turmoil, London luto Press), 1983.

Therborn, G., The Rule of Capital and the Rise of Democracy, in : ew Left Review, nr. 103, May-June 1977, pp. 3-41.

I

PART TWO:
PUBLIC CHOICE AND MACROECONOMIC POLICY

3 PUBLIC CHOICE THEORY AND MACROECONOMIC POLICY

Vani K Borooah

3.1. Introduction

The theme of this paper is Public choice theory and macroeconomic policy. Public choice has been defined as the "economic study of nonmarket decisionmaking or simply the application of economics to political science" (Mueller (1979) p.1). In this paper I will adopt a wider definition of public choice and define it as a study of the interaction between economic and political behaviour. In this wider form the subject is sometimes also referred to as "political economics" or "modern political economy". It is my belief that this wider definition is more appropriate for the purpose at hand, namely to study the relation between public choice and macroeconomics.

It is a truism that in societies characterised by democratic political systems, governments have periodically to submit themselves to the judgement of their electorates. All those who participate in democratic political processes have therefore an interest, first in identifying the factors that exert a significant influence on the electorate's judgement and second in manipulating these factors so as to elicit, for themselves, a favourable verdict from the electorate. The interaction between politics and economics lies in the fact that many of such factors are of an economic nature. In the words of Harold wilson, ex British Prime Minister "... all political history shows that the standing of a Government and its ability to hold the confidence of the electorate at a General Election depends upon the success of the economic policy." Let

Julien van den Broeck (ed.), Public Choice, 61-90.
© *1988 by Kluwer Academic Publishers and Association of Post-Keynesian Studies.*

me hasten to add that I do not for a moment believe that only economic factors weigh with voters or that these are even the most important of influences on their judgement. Anyone familiar with recent British history will know that events in the realm of defence and foreign affairs have had important electoral impacts. However to the extent that some of the important electoral influences are economic in nature, public choice theory may have some light to shed on the making of macroeconomic policy. A discussion of what the nature of this light might be forms the basis of the remainder of this paper.

3.2. Economic performance and political popularity

As noted earlier, one strand of the interaction between economics and politics lies in the hypothesis that there is a causal connection between a government's macroeconomic performance and its economic popularity. In turn this hypothesis has attracted the attention of both political scientists and economists. Public choice theory has much to say about voting, but from the point of view of this paper, perhaps two aspects can be singled out. The first is the logic of the voter. Why do (or do not) voters respond to economic issues? Do voters respond to certain issues but not to others? Do different voters respond differently to different issues and if so why? The answers to all these questions are of considerable importance to modern governments. Of no less importance is the second aspect which is the empirical counterpart to the first. What are the economic issues with which voters are concerned? Is it inflation, unemployment, real incomes? What is the relative strength of their concern with these issues? Does this relative ranking of issues vary with the type of voter being considered? The answers to such questions are of course not to be found in public choice theory, but rather in the testing of the theory against data.

Views on what constitutes the logic of the voter vary depending on the nature of the academic discipline from which it is being perceived. Thus some might argue that class loyalty is the basis for voting behaviour, others might argue that housing has an important influence and still others might say that perceptions of individual well being on the part of voters are a critical determinant of where their vote goes. From this melange of opinions, the view that has been adopted by public choice theory, since it has as its basis the rational economic man so beloved of standard economic theory, is that of Downs (1957).

In a Downsian world a voter is rational in the sense that he casts his vote for the party he believes will provide him with more benefits than any other. The benefits which may be many and various are reduced to a common denominator which Downs calls the "utility income" of government activity. To discover which party he would vote for, the individual voter compares his expected utility incomes from the various parties and casts his vote for the party from which he expects the highest utility income.

In making this comparison a voter must arrive at a judgement of what a party will actually do when it comes to power. For the incumbent party, its performance in the current period might offer some guide; for the parties in opposition however the voter would have to construct a hypothetical guide. Downs recognised however that collecting information for an inter-party evaluatory excercise might be a costly process and that therefore, for this reason, no voter would attempt a comprehensive evaluation. Instead each voter would base his evaluation upon those areas where the differences between the parties are sufficient to impress him. Thus the voter remains indifferent as to which party is in power until the inter-party difference in utility flows is large enough.

Within this context of rationality, an important question, to which public choice theory has no plausible answer, is why a voter should go to the trouble of voting when he knows that, in all probability, his vote would have no influence on the final outcome. To explain this one would have to step outside the framework of the egoistic individual, termed by Sen (1982) as the "rational fool" and posit instead a sense of duty and commitment as a motivational springboard for human action. Thus as Ashenfelter and Kelly (1975) in a study of the two US presidential elections of 1960 and 1972 note,

> "the theory of voting that is best supported by our results is that which posits a sense of duty or obligation as the primary motivation for voting" (p. 724)

Even in the casting of ones vote, as will be argued below, people may act out of sympathy for others and that the evaluation of utility streams may not be based entirely on egoistic considerations.

Thus Butler and Stokes (1974) argued, on the basis of survey data, that the state of the economy exerted its influence on the electorate's mood through essentially two channels. First there was the link between party support and perception of individual well being and second there was the link between party support and a more general perception - perhaps derived from the media - about the state of the economy. Party support operating through the former channel was of course consistent with the notion of egoistic voter behaviour. However the influence of the second channel implied a broader consideration, by voters, of what was politically and economically desirable.

Most empirical work in this area has however been based on aggregate data and therefore has been unable to sustain the distinction between perceptions of individual well being (sympathetic behaviour). In terms of testing the theory all that this, mainly econometric, work has succeeded in doing, is establishing a relationship between voting intentions and certain key indicators of macroeconomic performance. In other words in such econometric models, everyone, favoured say, a reduction in the inflation rate or unemployment rate without any consideration of whether, and by how much, they individually would be affected by such a reduction. This point will be returned to later on. The upshot of these studies, which estimated "popularity functions" access a variety of countries for a variety of time periods, was to establish a link between political popularity and macroeconomic outcomes, though the precise composition of these outcomes differed from study to study.

These studies based on the notion (either explicitly or implicitly) of an utility maximising voter and employing econometric techniques for the empirical analysis came under attack from the political science profession. In particular two major lines of criticism were advanced. Firstly it was argued that government popularity followed a cyclical pattern over the lifetime of a government, reaching a trough between elections and peaking at or before an election. Since this did not necessarily correspond to the cyclical pattern of economic variables, it was argued that the link between the two was not as strong as economists might believe. Indeed, it was further argued (cf. Miller and Mackie (1973)) that an alternative explanation for the existence of cycles in government popularity might be that the nature of the response to the question on voting intentions altered with the passage of time. Thus, when a general election was near, the nature of the response was likely to involve comparisons between the government and the opposition parties. On the other hand, away from a general election, the response was likely to be a non-comparative one and the incumbent party was likely to be more heavily penalised for its perceived shortcomings.

The second line of criticism was that even if economic affairs did exert an influence, the relevant determinants of popularity were voters' perceptions of economic performance. Yet almost all econometric studies employed as explanatory variables for changes in popularity, data series published by government statistical services. Thus a major area for research was the link between objective events and their reporting by the media and then between the media reports and the electorate's evaluation of governmental performance.

Notwithstanding such disquiet, the welter of economic results on this area has continued unabated with members of the political science profession, particular in the USA, also getting in on the act. Within this context of econometric analysis, two areas remain, in my view, relatively neglected. First, the relation between political popularity and economic performance does not appear to be a stable one. Indeed there is evidence that the electorate's criteria for judging the economic performance of a government changes over time and, in particular, changes between periods relating to different governments. The economic problems that are highlighted - and by implication the problems that are underplayed - differ between governments. This may be partly due to differences in ideology and partly due to a desire to take advantage of existing economic conditions. To some extent this alters voters percention of what is important; to another extent voters judge governments by the criteria governments themselves set. Both factors combine to produce changes even time in the criteria of economic success (cf. Borooah and van der Ploeg (1984) and Butler and Stokes (1974)).

The second area is one which Frans van Winden (1982) had done much to develop and that is the area of "interest groups". The idea that governments are rewarded for good times and punished for bad times assumes that voters are agreed on what constitutes good and bad times. In fact the most interesting issues in politics and economics are those on which voters, through differences of self interest, are divided (cf. Stigler (1973)). Thus for example the proposal that tax relief on mortgage interest should be removed would be of no personal concern to persons living in publicly provided housing but would greatly alarm owner occupiers of dwellings. From this division amongst voters follows quite naturally the idea of the formation of 'interest groups' by which attach themselves to the political parties the voters best see as representing their interests. The intensity of this attachment might increase in bad times (and decrease in good times) so that one consequence of economic hardship might not be a general reduction of support for the ruling party but an increase of support for each party in the class whose interests it represents and a decline in the support for each party in the class whose interests it does not represent (cf. Converse (1958)).

With these observations I would now like to turn to the question of whether it is possible for governments to manipulate economic events in order to secure an electoral advantage.

3.3. The politics of economic policy

Neither Marx nor Kalecki were strangers to the idea that the functioning of an economy can, and does, have a political basis. By emphasizing the role of class conflict, in the Marxian schema, the economy would be characterised by booms and slumps calculated "not only to leave intact the foundations of the capitalist system, but also to secure its reproduction on a progressive scale" (Marx (1967), vol. 1, p. 620). Kalecki argued that "the class instinct of business leaders tells them that lasting full employment is unsound from their point of view" and that therefore a government's economic policy would be directed towards ensuring that "unemployment is an integral part of the normal capitalist system" (Kalecki (1943)).

The existence of class conflict in society and its possible influence on economic policy and performance has however been studiously ignored by the dominant paradigm in economics.Indeed this paradigm, with its vision blinkered by the principle of optimizing behaviour, has been forced to examine questions of a purely normative, and empirically irrelevant, nature, namely the principles that ought to underlie the making of policy, and has had to eschew an investigation of the positive, and empirically relevant, issues, namely the principles that actually underlie, the making of policy.

In this normative, optimizing tradition the work of Tinbergen (1952) was seminal. In the Tinbergen approach the government was viewed as a benevolent dictator acting in the best interests of the governed and in operational terms its problem was to choose levels of policy instruments that would maximize a given social welfare function. Although this approach to economic policy was subsequently refined in several respects, the view of government acting for the greatest good of the governed remained unchanged until Nordhaus (1975) investigated the optimum policy required to maximize a government's re-election prospects subject to the constraint of an inflation-unemployment trade-off. However this attempt by Nordhaus to inject a degree of political realism into an analysis of government behaviour remained rooted in the normative, optimizing tradition (i.e. what should a government do to maximize its re-election prospects) and it was dissatisfaction with this tradition that led others, (Frey (1978a,b) Frey and Schneider (1978)), to seek an explanation of what governments actually do, in terms of 'satisfacing' rather than optimizing behaviour.

Almost a century after Marx, therefore, the wheel has turned full circle, and mainstream economists are expressing an (albeit peripheral) interest in the motivations that underlie the making of economic policy. With this renewed interest however, the insights provided by Marx and Kalecki in terms of societal conflict continue to be ignored and the analysis remains one of a situation in which a homogeneous entity governs a homogeneous society. It is the contention of this paper that no proper understanding of the behaviour of government, in its role as economic policy maker, is possible without taking account of the differences in interests between the various groups in society and that therefore, our understanding in this area has not been greatly advanced by either 'the optimizing' or 'satisficing' approaches to the making of economic policy.

3.4. Marxist views on the political business cycle

'The goal of macropolicy is not to eliminate the (business) cycle but to guide it in the interests of the capitalist class.' This quotation from Boddy and Crotty (1975, p. 10) summarises the modern Marxist view of the political business cycle. Marx's own view was that the conflict between labour and capital over their shares of the national income would lead to cyclical booms and slumps. In the expansionary phase of the cycle, unemployment would rise, the reserve army of the unemployed would diminish and workers would bargain successfully for higher shares of the rising national income. The counterpart of this would be a profits squeeze with the share of profits in national income falling. To end this decline in profits, capitalists would have to take steps to bring the expansionary phase of the cycle to a halt. This they would do by slowing down the rate of capital accumulation so that 'the movement of rise in wages receives a check. The rise of wages therefore is confined within the limits that not only leave intact the foundations of the capitalist system, but also secure its reproduction on a progressive scale' Marx, 1967, vol. I, p. 620).

Marx's view on the nature of the business cycle did not include the view that the operation of government policy itself generated cycles. In Marx's schema the generation of cycles was entirely in the power of the capitalist class. The recognition that government policies, through a manipulation of expenditure and taxes, would influence the level of employment had to await the birth of Keynesianism. With this recognition grew the assumption among Keynesians that one of the objectives of government policy was the maintenance of full employment in the economy, an assumption, which if true and if capable of being executed, would, of course, imply an end to business cycles.

This assumption was challenged by Kalecki who argued that

"the assumption that a government will maintain full employment in a capitalist economy if it only knows how to do it is fallacious... the maintenance of full employment would cause social and political changes which would give a new impetus to the opposition of business leaders... the class instinct of [business leaders] tells them that lasting full employment is unsound from their point of view and that unemployment is an integral part of the normal capitalist system (Kalecki, 1943 , pp. 138-139 and pp. 140-141)."

Although Kalecki's views were grounded in Marx's theories of class conflict, Kalecki's reasons for the basis of the conflict were more social than economic. Thus Kalecki argued that the businessman's dislike of continued full employment was based on the fear that under such a regime the self-assurance of the working classes, who could not be fired from their jobs, would grow, with a consequent undermining of the social position of the bosses. In fact, in terms of economic (as opposed to social) self-interest businessmen had no reason to fear continued full employment, for under Kalecki's theory of monopoly pricing businesses could maintain profit margins under full-employment conditions. The implications of the above argument for business cycles was that governments would attempt to maintain full employment but would retreat from this policy whenever periods of high employment were sufficiently protracted to arouse the opposition of the capitalist class.

More recently the orthodox Marxist view of business cycles being generated through class conflict based on a clash of economic interests has been resurrected by Boddy and Crotty (1975). In their analysis, the main concern of capitalists is assumed to be the maximisation of profits and they argue on the basis of post-World War II evidence that macropolicy has served the interests of the capitalist class, that is to say, macropolicy has aided and abetted capitalists in their primary aim of profit maximisation. Organised labour, on the other hand, has merely served as a constraint to the pursuit of the economic interests of the capitalists. Business cycles, in turn, are generated by the twin phenomena of macropolicy serving capitalists and organised labour seeking to constrain this service.

This thesis is based upon the observation that profits are at their highest in the earlier part of the expansion. In the latter part of the expansion, profits come under severe pressure and indeed profits continue to decline during the contraction, thereby sowing the seeds for the destruction of the boom period. Thus, although in an ideal world capitalists would like to avoid recession, a recession is a necessary stage for attaining the high profit first phase of the expansion and also for avoiding the sustained full-employment dangers of the second phase of the expansion. This view is illustrated in Fig. 1 where as the economy moves from recovery to boom (the first and second phases of the expansion) the share of wages in value added falls, reaching a minimum at the turning point. In the boom phase the share of wages rises and continues to rise through the first phase of the recession and is only made to fall when the second phase of the recession is reached. The above story is very similar to an alternative class struggle interpretation of the business cycle (see Goodwin, 1967; van der Ploeg, 1982), which assumes full capacity utilisation. In this alternative framework capitalists can undermine the power of the workers by withdrawing machinery and demand for labour during a profit squeeze, but in the case of under-utilisation the capitalists need to be aided by the government to check the bargaining strength of unions (cf. Boddy and Crotty, 1975). A glance at the development of the world economy during the years 1979-82 provides casual evidence for the Marxist view. During the late sixties and seventies most of the capitalist countries experienced a wages explosion, the strength of trade unions increased and the share of profits was squeezed. The resulting inflation and public sector deficits provided an ideal argument for Western European governments - including the 'socialist' governments of Mitterand and Schmidt - to deflate the economy. Detailed evidence on the Marxist view is provided by Feiwel (1974) and Boddy and Crotty (1975).

Fig. 1   A Marxist view of the political business cycle

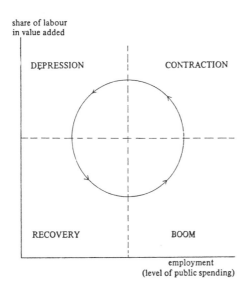

The Marxist view of business cycles is 'political' in a broad sense in that the mechanism generating the cycles is class conflict based on conflict over the division of economic spoils, with the government aiding the capitalist class and organised labour constraining their ability to do so. The more recent theories of political business cycles adopt a narrower perspective on the political process and depend for the generation of cycles upon the desire of governments, in democratic societies, to be re-elected. It is to such theories that we now turn.

3.5. Optimizing approaches to the political business cycle

After Kalecki's classical contribution to understanding the political business cycle, there was a long period of neglect of the political aspect of economic policy formulation. The revival of interest in the political business cycle was due to Nordhaus (1975). However, Nordhaus did not present this theory in terms of a struggle between social classes but instead focused on the short-run trade-off between inflation and unemployment. The context of this shift in emphasis was the debate in the 1960s and early 1970s about how vertical the price-expectations augmented Phillips curve was and by how much the short-run Phillips curve could be shifted.

The basic behavioural assumption in the Nordhaus model, was that the electorate was only concerned about the level of unemployment and the rate of inflation and its support (or lack of support) for the government depended only upon the outcome of these two variables. This meant that events in the economy relating to, for example, real incomes, balance of payments, social security benefits etc. were ignored and also that divisions within the electorate along, say class lines, were irrelevant in determining the governments support level. The government, for its part, was then assumed to follow policies, that, given the preferences of the electorate, would guarantee its re-election. Under these assumptions, Nordhaus showed that the optimal outcome would be a political business cycle of the following form.

Immediately after an election the government follows policies to raise the level of unemployment which in turn lowers the rate of inflation and depresses inflationary expectations. The rationale for such a policy is that it is an 'investment" in the future which shifts the short run Phillips curve closer to the origin in the latter years of the government's life. Closer to the next election policies are followed which reduce the level of unemployment at the expense of an increase in the actual inflation rate; however since the Phillips curve has been shifted inwards the inflation rate associated with the reduced unemployment level is not as great as it would have been if the post election 'investment' had not been undertaken. Thus on election eve the government secures a low level of unemployment in conjunction with a moderate' rate of inflation and after securing re-election repeats the cycle which is illustrated in Fig. 2.

Fig. 2   The optimal political business cycle

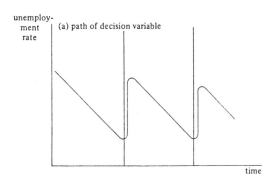

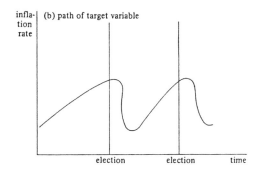

Apart from the restrictiveness of the behavioural assumptions relating to the electorate - whereby it, as a homogeneous entity, cares only about unemployment and inflation - the existence of Nordhaus' business cycle depends upon the further assumption that voters are backward looking and never contemplate the consequences of government policy; as a consequence they never anticipate that hard times follow good times which leads to the cycle being perpetuated.

If, more reasonably, it was assumed that the electorate not only knew its likes and dislikes but also understood and took account of politically motivated economic policy, then this could prevent the appearance of the political business cycle a la Nordhaus. By penalising the government for its cyclical policies, the electorate could ensure through strategic voting, that the economy was always characterised by low levels of unemployment and relatively high rates of inflation.

Nordhaus (1975), in a survey of 9 countries, conceded that, over 1947-72, there was no evidence for his political business cycle in Australia, Canada, Japan and the United Kingdom, very modest evidence for France and Sweden and reasonable evidence for only Germany, New Zealand and the USA. Macrae (1977) cast further doubts on the empirical relevance of Nordhaus' model, by showing that for the USA evidence for the political business cycle was confined to the Kennedy and Johnson years and that there was no evidence for such a cycle during the Eisenhower and Nixon administrations.

3.6. Satisficing approaches to the formulation of economic policy

The empirical irrelevance of the Nordhaus (1975) model is not surprising, since there are strong reasons that might prevent governments from behaving as predicted. The derivation of optimal political-economic strategies is, in mosts practical situations, complicated and cannot expect a government to be able to 'optimize on the economy'. This difficulty is of course compounded if the government does not possess the required information or is faced with conflicting views on the behaviour of the economy and the electorate. Consequently, the formulation of ex ante economic policy is, for most governments, a questionable proposition. Instead, a government is more likely to carry on with established policies until a crisis arises, when it might modify or abandon existing policies in response to the crisis. This ex post formulation of economic policy may be found in the 'feedback' approach to the theory of economic policy (cf. Tustin (1954), Philips (1954) though the approaches there are typically normative, whereas the purpose of political economics is to provide a positive explanation of economic behaviour.

Reacting to these criticisms Frey (1978a, b) and Frey and Schneider 1978) put forward a satisficing model of government behaviour which ran as follows: the primary objective of a government was to promote its ideology. However, in order to pursue this objective a government must remain in office and a political crisis would exist for the government if re-election was judged unlikely. Consequently, in the absence of a political crisis a government would implement its ideology and in the presence of a political crisis a government would follow 'popular' policies. The criteria to judge whether a given situation represented a political crisis would of course be flexible, since low popularity is less serious just after an election than just prior to an election.

In the light of these comments, it has been suggested that a government may adjust its policy instruments (taxes, subsidies, public spending etc.) according to a threetier political economic reaction function (e.g. Frey, 1978a, b, or Frey and Schneider, 1978). The first component is only active when there is a popularity deficit and usually involves reflationary measures such as cutting taxes or implementing public works. The implicit assumption underlying such a strategy is that the popularity deficit is caused by too high unemployment or a too low growth in disposable income rather than a balance of payments crisis or too much inflation, since the latter two factors would require deflationary measures. In other words such a simple vote-satisficing strategy typically fails to take account of the cause of the popularity crisis. The second component of the political-economic reaction function is active when there is scope for discretionary policy, that is when there is a popularity surplus. A Conservative administration may cut public spending and taxes, whereas a Labour government may take the opportunity to increase taxes to finance an expansion of the state. The third component of the political-economic policy rule is active regardless of the government's popularity, since it captures purely economic factors. For example, the unemployment benefit component of public spending may rise when the unemployment level or, assuming that the benefit rate is related to the private sector wage rate, average earnings rise.

In the next two sections we argue that, although such a positive approach is an improvement over earlier normative approaches it cannot explain a major contemporary phenomenon namely the rise in government expenditures, over the past two decades, in countries of the OECD. After a brief review of public expenditure trends in the UK, it is then argued that much of this rise can be understood by appreciating the role of conflict between government departments.

3.7. Public expenditure in the UK : recent trends

The most striking fact about trends in public expenditure in the United Kingdom, is the rise in such expenditures, both in real terms and as a percentage of GDP, over the past two decades. In 1960, the real value of general government expenditure (at 1980 GDP prices) was £50 billion, by 1985 it had more than doubled to reach £113 billion. Fig. 3 illustrates those changes. Over this 25 year period, general government expenditures grew at an average annual rate of 3.33 per cent; the corresponding growth in real GDP was 2.28 per cent. Although the annual rate of growth of general government expenditures and GDP varied over the period 1960-85 (see Table 1), the former growth rate consistently outstripped the latter.

As a percentage of GDP, general government expenditure rose from 35 per cent in 1960 to a peak of 48 per cent in 1975. After the cuts imposed as a consequence of the financial crisis of 1976, it fell to 42

Fig. 3

General government expenditure in real terms,[a] 1960-85

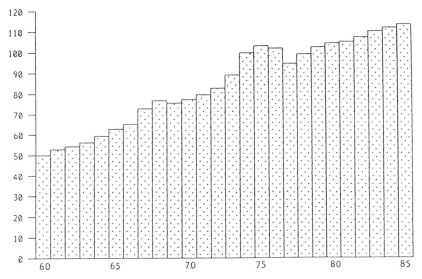

[a]Cash figures deflated using GDP deflator, 1980 = 100

Source: Economic Trends Annual Supplement (ETAS) 1987.

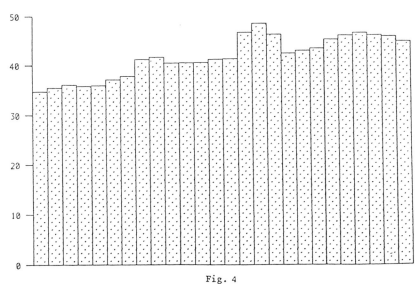

Fig. 4

General government expenditure as a percentage of GDP[a]

[a]At market prices

Source: ETAS 1987.

Table 1

Public Expenditure Outturn in Relation to Plan

	Planning Total		£ billion actual prices	
	Plan	Outturn	Difference	% of Plan
1972-73	27.2	27.4	0.2	0.74
1973-74	31.7	32.6	0.9	2.8
1974-75	39.8	43.3	3.5	8.8
1975-76	49.6	51.2	1.6	3.2
1976-77	58.7	56.2	-2.5	-4.2
1977-78	60.5	57.6	-2.9	-4.8
1978-79	66.4	66.1	-0.3	0.5
1979-80	75.1	77.1	2.0	2.7
1980-81	91.1	93.5	2.4	2.6
1981-82	104.4	105.3	0.9	0.9
1982-83	114.7	113.1	-1.6	1.4
1983-84	119.6	120.4	0.8	0.7
1984-85	126.5	128.2	1.7	1.3
1985-86	132.1	134.2	2.1	1.6
1986-87	139.1	140.4	1.3	0.9

'Plan' refers to the figures published in the public expenditure
White Paper immediately preceding the year in question.

Source : Wright (1978) up to 1974-75, Ward (1983) up to
1981-82 and Public Expenditure White Paper,
January 1987 thereafter

per cent in 1977. Thereafter it again rose, reaching a peak of 46
percent over the years 1981-83, since when it has somewhat fallen.
Fig. 4 illustrates these movements. However underlying this rising trend,
are differential rates of growth in the different items of public
expenditure. The major items of growth in the past 8 years have been
social security transfers and spending on defence and health and
personal social services; the items to suffer have been spending on
public housing and subsidies to industry. An analysis of the economic
categories of spending reveals that wages and salaries are, apart from
transfers, a major component of public spending. Thus public sector pay
and employment policies are a crucial element in the determination of
public expenditure. Although manpower levels in the public sector have
fallen by 13 per cent since 1978-79, public sector pay over the period
1978 tot 1986 increased in real terms by over 16 per cent.

A comparison with other OECD countries shows that this experience
was not unique: between 1960 and 1982 all OECD countries recorded a
rise in their ratio of public expenditure to GDP. The position of the UK
in the OECD's public expenditure league has also altered. In 1960 only 2
countries France (34.6 per cent) and the Netherlands (33.7 per cent)
exceeded the UK's percentage of public expenditure to GDP (32.6 per
cent). By 1982 the UK figure of 47.4 per cent was exceeded by 11
OECD countries.

The rise of public expenditure in OECD countries is therefore a
major contemporary phenomenon and one that public choice theory in its
traditional form has been unable to come to grips with. As we have
seen, different components of public expenditure have grown at different
rates and econometric investigations into the political business cycle
literature, constrained as they are by considering public expenditure in
aggregate, miss this point. This therefore argues for a much more
disaggregated approach to explaining the general rise in government
expenditure. I will not dwell on this point here but a glance at Fig. 5
will illustrate my point.

My second point is that, certainly for the UK, one cannot
appreciate the rise in public spending without understanding the process

Fig. 5   Public Spending by Function

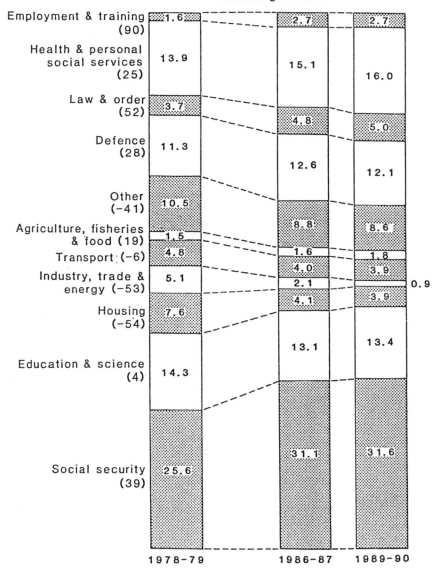

Percentage Shares

Source : Public Expenditure White Paper, January 1987.
Reproduced by kind permission of HMSO

of public expenditure determination. A study of this process for the UK
brings out very sharply the role of conflict between the different
government departments in planning public expenditure. The outcome is a
resolution of this conflict and frequently therefore this gives the
impression that public expenditure is "out of control". This point is
examined in some detail below.

3.8. Organisational explanations

The explanations for the growth of public expenditure that have the
narrowest focus are those which concentrate on the behaviour of the
protagonists in the public expenditure planning process. Perhaps the best
description of this process is provided by Jenkins (1985) who writes that
it "is the nearest that modern Whitehall gets to war. The campaign
season is brief, from July to October. The protagonists are always the
same, the Treasury and the spending departments. But the outcome is
never predictable. At the end of each year the participants agree there
must be a better way of settling the issue. Yet the following summer
the season opens with the procedure unreformed".

The basis for the dispute is the Treasury's public expenditure survey
committee (PESC) which is an interdepartmental group composed of
departmental finance officers and Treasury officials and chaired by a
Treasury deputy secretary. The origins of PESC lie in the Plowden
report of 1961 on the Control of Public Expenditure which recommended
that arrangements should be made to carry out surveys of public
expenditure for a number of years ahead and that all major decisions
involving new expenditure should be taken against the background of such
a survey. The purpose of PESC followed from this recommendation and
it was to create an annual review procedure, encompassing the whole of
the public sector, for a number of years ahead, which broke down
expenditure by function and by economic category and which therefore
enabled the spending of different departments to be co-ordinated and
also enabled public expenditure to be integrated into overall economic

policy. However, notwithstanding the merits of its conception, "the PESC round", in practice, has proved to be, under both Labour and Conservative governments, the focus of confrontation between Treasury parsimony and the expenditure ambitions of the spending ministers.

Each summer, the Treasury provides the Cabinet with its recommended planning total for the forward survey period; this total provides the basis for negotiations between the Treasury and the spending departments through the summer. The forum for these negotiations is usually one or the other of the half dozen or so Cabinet committees. Earlier, any disputes that were not settled at the Committee stage were taken to Cabinet for a final decision, but as the result of an innovation in 1981 they are now taken before a special committee - dubbed the "Star chamber". By adjudicating such disputes the "Star chamber" forestalls, though does not prevent, a Minister claiming his right to appeal to full Cabinet. When all conflicts between the Treasury and the spending departments have been resolved, the Government publishes a Public Expenditure White Paper setting out its expenditure plans for the next 3-4 years. With its publication, the public expenditure planning process is drawn to a close for the year.

The organisational explanation for the growth of public expenditure in the UK is that the system for planning and controlling such expenditure is "out of control" in that whatever the level of expenditure planned and approved by ministers, PESC is unable to ensure that the outturn of expenditure does not exceed the planned level. Table 1 compares the outturn of public expenditure in relation to plan for each year for the period 1972-73 to 1986-87. This shows that the outturns for the 3 years, 1972-73 , 1973-74 and 1974-75, consistently exceeded their planned levels. Indeed the discrepancy between the outturn for 1974-75 and the level planned for that year became known as the "missing billions" and acquired a certain notoriety at that time, both in Parliament and in the Press. The introduction of cash limits in 1976, however, reversed this situation for the next 3 years, and till 1978-79, the outturn for public spending was below the planned level. More recently however, the tendency to overspend appears to have been estored. Fig. 5 provides some evidence therefore that one reason for he growth of public expenditure in the UK has been the failure to nsure that planned levels of expenditure were adhered to. Over the 15 ear period 1972-73 till 1986-87 only 4 years were characterised by nderspending; of these,the IMF's strictures were responsible for inderspending, through the introduction of cash limits, in the period 978-77 till 1978-79.

To understand why public expenditure plans were, almost .lways, exceeded in their outturn, one has to distinguish between the ore-1976 system of planning in terms of the volume of expenditure and he current practice, which began in 1976, of "cash limits". Before 1976, oublic expenditures were planned for in real terms over the planning norizon of 4-5 years, the main aim being to plan the provision of given levels of public goods and services against a background of orecasts about the future availability of resources. However, as a consequence of its emphasis on planning in volume terms, PESC was unable to control expenditure in money terms. In particular the 1973 oil orice rise combined with militant wage demands and high interest rates meant that given volumes of public services had to be provided at much greater monetary costs than was anticipated. In evidence to the Select Committee on Expenditure, Wynnen Godley stated "the emphasis on trying to control expenditure in real terms has meant that the control of the money has to a large extent gone by default. Departments have, as it were, been able to bill the Treasury for increases in pay, simply like that". (1st Report, 1975-76).

If real public expenditures and GDP were projected to grow at the same rate, differential productivity growth between the public and private sectors of the economy would ensure that the money value of public expenditure would increase as a proportion of GDP. This so called "relative price effect" occurs because, while productivity gains offset to some extent the rising cost of labour in the private sector,it is conventionally assumed that there is no productivity growth associated with the public provision of goods and services. There is of course nothing inevitable about the "relative price effect" which relies for its operation on the assumption that, in spite of differential productivity growth, wage growth in the public and private sectors is the same. Thus the effect can be frustrated by governments deciding to hold wage growth in the public sector below private sector levels. However most governments in the UK had decided that the political costs of trying to achieve this were too great to justify the attempt.

Exacerbating the relative price effect has been the fact that, in the UK, real GDP growth has consistently been outstripped by growth in the real value of public expenditure (cf. Fig. 4). One reason for this is that while public expenditure has been planned to grow at the same rate as GDP, the projected growth of the British economy has frequently been over-optimistic. Thus for example, in 1963, within 2 years of the inception of PESC, public expenditure over the period 1963-67 was planned to grow at the rate of 4 percent, which was projected growth rate of GDP; in the event this latter projection proved widely unrealistic. This habit of planning expenditure on the basis of unrealistic expectations of economic growth was not confined to Labour governments - the Heath government in 1972 projected an annual economic growth rate, over 1973-76, of 3.5 per cent and planned public expenditure accordingly. In the event the actual growth rate of the economy over the period was -0.3 per cent.

A weakness of PESC was that when expectations of economic growth, that would "pay for" increases in public expenditure, were not fulfilled it proved impossible to cut-back on such expenditure. An inherent difficulty with PESC was that commitments made in years 1 and 2 were firm with expenditure alterations only possible from year 3 onwards. As a consequence governments contemplating cuts in public expenditure tended to cut planned expenditure for years 3, 4 and 5. However, as the plans were revised and rolled forward, the cuts were restored and, in turn, future plans were reduced. Criticising this profile of public expenditure, the Select Committee on Expenditure noted that a 1 per cent reduction in public expenditure planned in the 1975 budget or the period 1975-76 and 1976-77, was transformed into a $2\frac{1}{2}$ per cent increase in the public expenditure White Paper a year later.

In any event by 1975 it was acknowledged by the Treasury that the monetary cost of public expenditure was out of control. The solution proposed was to change to a system of "cash limits" and such a system was introduced in 1976. A "cash limit" is defined as "an administrative limit on the amount of cash that the government proposes to spend on certain services, or blocks of services". Under the new system PESC planning allocations between programmes continued to be made on a volume basis, for a number of years ahead; the difference was that now, year 1 figures for all departmental programmes were converted into cash figures, and these represented "limits" or "planned ceilings" for these programmes. The only programmes excluded from "cash limits" were demand determined ones - mainly social security payments - and, as a proportion of total public sector expenditure, such exclusions amounted to about 38 per cent. Of equal importance as "cash limits" was the setting up of a monitoring system to enable the Treasury to identify areas of overspending before it was too late to take corrective action.

After 1976 therefore, there was a change of emphasis from the planning of public expenditure to the control of public expenditure. The presumption now was that any incompatibility between the planned provision of services and cash limits would have to be resolved by cut-backs in services. Since cash limits were derived by applying an "expected" inflation rate to volume levels, an underestimation of the inflation rate would represent an additional squeeze on public expenditure over and above any restraint planned as a result of the normal PESC review. Any government which was interested in controlling inflation would have an incentive to bias downwards the inflation allowance embodied in the cash limits. Likierman (1983) shows that for 3 of the 6 years of the period 1976-77 to 1981-82, the actual inflation rate exceeded the inflation allowance by 3 per cent or more.

Overall, cash limits resulted in significant shortfalls in expenditure, relative to planned levels, in the first 3 years of their inception, i.e. over the period 1976-77 till 1978-79. Since 1979 however, the outturn has exceeded planned levels. This reflects not so much a failure of control as the fact that it is difficult to restrain public expenditure in a time of falling activity. As noted earlier demand determined components of public expenditure - comprising 38 per cent of the total - were exempt from cash limits. The recession of 1980 which, within a year, doubled unemployment levels to 3 million (as against the planned level of 1.8 million for 1981-82) added over £1.5 billion to expenditure. In addition, to combat the worst effects of the recession the government was forced to lend large sums to nationalised industries and to spend on various employment measures - two areas in which it had planned to achieve a considerable cut-back in its expenditure.

The system of cash limits has survived the 11 years since its inception in 1976. Although since 1979 public expenditure plans have been consistently exceeded the breach has been the result of items not subject to cash limits and by and large, cash limits on the various expenditure blocks have held up. However the prognosis for the future is generally regarded as poor. This is for three reasons. First, cash limits have been used to influence public sector pay settlements by including in their announcement a budgeted pay figure. However in each year the actual pay settlement has exceeded the budgeted figure, thus damaging the credibility of cash limits. Moreover, the reduction in the volume of public services required to stay within the cash limits, as a consequence or this breach, has so far not proved unacceptable. There is no guarantee that this will continue to hold in future particularly if the gap between the pre-specified inflation rate and the actual inflation rate becomes too great. Second, the success of cash limits has been at the expense of capital expenditure and since 1976 the conditions of the public sector capital stock has undeniably deteriorated. Any attempt however to reverse this neglect will place an additional strain on the system. Finally, the weakness of cash limits is that any flexibility in their implementation is liable to be interpreted as a licence to overspend; the credibility of cash limits therefore depends upon their rigid enforcement. This is particularly important when it is remembered that there do not appear to be any sanctions that can be imposed on those who breach their cash limits.

Any statement of the problems of controlling public expenditure in the UK must necessarily be incomplete unless it alludes to the problem of controlling local authority expenditure, which in 1986-87, constituted about 28 percent of the public expenditure planning total. The Treasury in its desire to control expenditure is motivated by macroeconomic considerations.

Local authorities, on the other hand, do not share this concern to the same degree; at the same time they are statutorily obliged to provide certain services, regardless of the size of demand for such services. In meeting this demand, the electoral popularity of he party controlling a particular local council, depends crucially on the quality of the service provided. These considerations often bring the spending aims of local authorities into conflict with Treasury parsimony.

The main Treasury weapon for controlling local authority expenditure the Rate Support Grant (RSG) - was not designed to fill the gap between local authority expenditure and local authority taxes ("rates"); its purpose was to help the poorer authorities who could not raise much revenu from rates. More recently however, the Treasury has attempted to control local authority expenditure by cuts in the RSG in conjunction with a policy or "rate capping", i.e. of imposing a ceiling on the revenue raised through rates. The failure of this method has revealed that the control of local authorities ultimately rests on their voluntary compliance with the Treasury's expenditure guide-lines.

9. Concluding Remarks

This paper attempted to examine the interaction between events in the political and economic spheres and the role of such interaction in determining macroeconomic policy. The first part of this paper analysed the proposition that a government's macroeconomic policies and outcomes significantly affected its electoral popularity. Studies in this area indicate that this proposition is not without support though there is some debate among investigators as to the nature of the economic factors that affect this relationship.

Two areas in this field that are relatively neglected are stability analysis and differences in voter self interests. Both these areas have interesting economic implications and any realistic attempt to assess the electoral impact of macroeconomic policy must take these features into account.

The second, and substantially longer, part of this paper was concerned with the possibility of macroeconomic policy being manipulated in order to secure political advantage. The literature on this theme has a fairly long and distinguished pedigree - neither Marx nor Kalecki were strangers to the idea that the functioning of an economy can, and does have a political basis. Their views were political in a broad sense in that the basis of interaction between the economy and the polity lay in class conflict between capitalists and workers, with government aiding the capitalist class and workers constraining their ability to do so. This insight regarding the importance of societal conflict in determining the course of the economy has unfortunately been ignored by mainstream economists which have instead sought to seek the interaction between politics and economics within the more narrow confines of electoral behaviour. This has meant that public choice theory has been unable to explain a major contemporary phenomenon, namely the rise of publuc expenditure among countries of the OECD.

The paper concluded by attempting to demonstrate that the notion of conflict when applied to inter-ministerial conflict could go some way towards explaining the rise of public expenditure in the UK. Of course, such an explanation is only partial and is swamped by demographic and social effects, but is nevertheless a more plausible explanation (within the public choice framework) than conventional public choice theories.

References

Ashenfelter, O. and S. Kelley (1975), "Determinants of Participation in Presidential Elections", Journal of Law and Economics, vol. 18, pp

)5-733.

Boddy, R. and J. Crotty (1975), "Determinants of Participation in residential Elections", Journal of Law and Economics, vol. 18, pp.)5-733.

Borooah, V. K and F. van der Ploeg (1982), Political Aspects of the conomy, Cambridge University Press, Cambridge.

Butler, D. and D. Stokes (1974), Political Change in Britain, acmillan, London.

Converse,P.E. (1958), "The Shifting Role of Class in Political ttitudes and Behaviour", in E.E. Maccoby, T.M. Newcomb and E.L. artley (edited), Readings in Social Psychology, Methuen, London.

Downs, A. (1957), An Economic Theory of Democracy, Harper and op, New York.

Feiwel, G.R. (1974), 'Reflections on Kalecki's theory of the political usiness cycle", Kyklos, vol. 27, pp. 21-48.

Frey, B.S. (1978a), 'Politico-economic models and cycles', Journal of ublic Economics, vol. 9, pp. 203-220.

Frey, B.S. (1978b), Modern Political Economy, Martin Robertson, xford.

Frey, B.S. and F. Schnieder (1978), 'A politico-economic model of ne United Kingdom', Economic Journal, vol. 88, pp. 243-253.

Goodwin, R.M. (1967), 'A growht cycle", in C.H. Feinstein (ed.), ocialism, Capitalism and Economic Growth (Essays in honour of Maurice obb), Cambridge University Press, Cambridge.

Jenkins, S. (1985), "The 'Star Chamber", PESC and the Cabinet", olitical Quarterly, vol. 56,pp. 113-121.

Kalecki, M. (1943), , Political Quarterly, October/December, pp. 22-331. Also reprinted in Essays on the Dynamics of the Capitalist conomy, 1933-1970, Cambridge University Press, Cambridge.

Macrae, D. (1977), 'A Political model of the business cycle', Journal f Political Economy, vol. 85, pp.239-263.

Marx, K. (1967), Capital, Volumes I, II, III, International Publishers, ew York.

Miller, W.L. and M. Mackie, "The Electoral Cycle and the Asymmetry of Government and Opposition Popularity: an Alternative Model of the Relationship between Economic Conditions and Political Popularity", Political Studies, vol. 21, pp. 263-279.

Mueller, D.C. (1979), Public Choice, Cambridge University Press Cambridge.

Nordhaus, W.D. (1975), 'The political business cycle', Review of Economic Studies, volo. 42,pp. 169-190.

Phillips, A.W. (1954), 'Stabilization policy in a closed economy' Economic Journal, vol.64, pp. 2900-322.

Ploeg, F. van der (1982), 'Economic growth and conflict over the distribution of income', presented to the 1982 European Meeting of the Econometric Society, Dublin, forthcoming in the Journal of Economi Dynamics and Control.

Sen, A.K. (1982), 'The Rational Fool', in F.H. Hahn and M. Holli (edited), Philosophy and Economics.

Stigler, G.J. (1973), "General Economic Conditions and National Elections", American Economic Review, vol. 63, pp. 160-167.

Tinbergen, J. (1952), On the Theory of Economic Policy North-Holland, Amsterdam.

Tustin, A. (1954), The Mechanism of Economic Systems, Heinemann London.

van Winden, F. (1982), On the Interaction between State and Private Sector, North Holland, Amsterdam.

Ward, T. (1983), "PESC in Crisis", Policy and Politics, vol. 11, pp 167-176.

Wright, M. (1978), "Public Expenditure in Britain: the Crisis of Control", Public Administration, Summer, pp. 143-169.

PUBLIC CHOICE AND MACROECONOMIC POLICY
A Comment on Vani K Borooah

Dirk Heremans

4.1. Introduction

In this contribution the author, who has already widely published on political economics, raises many interesting issues on the complexity of interaction between political and economic behaviour. It corresponds to the needs to model the policymakers decision making process more realistically, especially in the macro economics field.

As also Dr. van Winden has pointed out in his survey it certainly is the merit of public choice that it has opened up the possibility of integrated political economic models that establish a link between political institutions and macroeconomic policy outcomes. There are, however, different ways to proceed to such an integration.

First, one can branch out from public choice theory and introduce some macroeconomic variables, mostly on a ad hoc basis, as determining the political decision making process. This approach has become popular in the construction and testing of so-called popularity functions, to which also Dr. Borooah refers.

Second, the alternative approach starts at the other end. It concentrates on macroeconomic modelbuilding and introduces public choice theory to explain the behaviour of individuals and policymakers. It turns out to be the more difficult route. Only recently a small but growing literature on this interaction is emerging in the novel macroeconomic approach of what has been labelled : "credibility and politics".

Julien van den Broeck (ed.), Public Choice, 91-101.
© *1988 by Kluwer Academic Publishers and Association of Post-Keynesian Studies.*

In addition another characteristic distinguished the two appraoches The first remains within the traditional macroeconomic framework of discretionary policy making. The second mostly adopts the new rationa expectations macroeconomic framework, and by implication devotes more attention to the structural and institutional aspects of the decision making process.

The contribution of Dr. Borooah limits itself to the first approach. It concentrates on the public decision making process without elaborating on formal macroeconomic modelbuilding. The paper starts out by criticising current public choice theory and provides some interesting hints as how an alternative research stragegy in terms of group conflicts might proceed. As the arguments draw mainly upon previous work by the author, and are surveyed rather summarily, I will also limit myself to some rather general observations on these issues. It could not be the purpose of this comment to review the whole of Dr. Borooah's contributions in the field.

A second and more specific contribution of the paper consists in an attempt to explain the rising trend of public expenditures in the U.K. The focus thereby is on the organisation of the budgetary process, involving many conflictual issues.

Before commenting upon these more specific issues it may be of interest to elaborate somewhat upon the alternative and more novel approach. The literature on "credibility and politics" can be seen as an attempt to arbitrage between the public choice and the recent macroeconomic literature. Moreover, one has to keep in mind that this arbitrage builts upon an earlier fruitful arbitrage between macroeconomic theory and the game theoretical industrial organisation theory (Alesina and Tabellini, 1987).

4.2. Macroeconomic policy and public choice : an alternative approach

In order to clarify the alternative approach, it is useful to start from a broader view on th links between macroeconomic policy and public choice theory. There is no need to emphasize further the present state of confusion in the area of macroeconomic policy-making, since the failure of Keynesian fine tuning and anticyclical stabilisation policies in the seventies. The public choice views certainly have strenghtened the ising criticism on the hydraulic Keynesian policy-prescriptions by monetarists and rational expectations theorists.

At first sight one may witness a certain policy convergence between recent macroeconomic theory and public choice. Both rational expectations and public choice theory find their roots in a further elaboration of the micro-economic foundations of macrobehaviour. Rational expectations reacts against the view of the behaviour of the private sector consisting of merely programmed role players in an hydraulic Keynesian world in which the government simply has to pull the levers. It also highlights the importance of the institutional environment as to the formation of expectations. Public choice theory can be seen as a reaction against the traditional Pigou-Keynes view of an anonymous government automatically acting in the general interest. In its microeconomic view of the government it points to the individual decision makers steering the collective decision making process to serve their own interest. Both theories then lead to a critical view of government policies and advocate (constitutional) rules to limit the discretionary power of governments. The policy implication is that economic policy should be drawn away from the daily operating level to the more important task of setting (medium term) policy rules and policy regimes.

However, this policy convergence does not rest upon the same analysis : the underlying views of how effective policies may be carried out and how individuals react to these policies substantially differ. According to public choice theory governments may reap short term electoral benefits by exploiting the political business cycle by discretionary policies that can be effectively implemented. In the rational expectations view, private agents anticipate government policies and thereby render policy changes - unless brought about by surprise - completely ineffective (the so-called policy ineffectiveness critique of

Lucas). The room for exploiting macroeconomic policies for electoral advantage is much more limited. Hence, similar preferences of both theories for (constitutional) rules are differently founded : in public choice theory on the possible exploitation of myopic voters by politicians aiming at reelection; in rational expectations on the well-informed voter who anticipates policies. His expectations and behaviour can only be stabilized by setting policies on a medium term course by adhering to preannounced rules.

Hence, analytically the assumption about information of the individual voter is the crucial issue. Whether he is forward or backward looking, determines whether his behaviour is co-determined by the anticipation of government policies. More importantly, this discussion highlights the lack of general macroeconomic models with endogenous government behaviour.

We must acknowledge that there have been efforts, also by Dr Borooah in one of his previous publications, to integrate public choice elements in a more traditional macromodel based upon adaptive expectations (Borooah and Van der Ploeg, 1983). In this respect, however the more recent developments within the framework of reputation models look more promising. They make the link between political institutions and national expectations macroeconomics explicit by focusing on the "reputation" of policymakers, that will both determine the effectiveness of macro-economic policies and the electoral outcomes. They may help to understand better the economic realities of the last decade, in particular the paradox that seemingly unpopular policies have strengthened the political appeal of governments in recent elections.

This novel approach on "credibility and politics" views policymaking as a game between policymakers and private agents in the economy. The analysis is carried out within the framework of small macroeconomic models specifying objectives and incentives for the policymakers together with constraints, such as political institutions, upon the actions of the players.

The explicit consideration of political constitutions in these macro-models raises several novel issues. First it focuses on the time in)consistency of optimal macroeconomic policies. It may create credibility problems due to the fact that the ex post constraints that governments face are different from the ex ante constraints. Second, it raises the question as to the desirability of commitments to policy rules. In this respect the role of policymakers' reputation in establishing credibility for their policy plans may be an alternative.

The models also allow to take into account the interaction between rather short-sighted politicians and long-sighted political parties. As to the preference functions of politicians and political parties two classes of models can be further distinguished. First, the models in which parties maximize popularity with reelection being the sole objective. Second, models in which different parties represent the interest of different constituencies with conflicting economic interests.

The exploration of these models has just begun, much work remains to be done to enrich the assumptions and to subject them to empirical testing. It looks a promising development, but it certainly would be premature to draw final conclusions (Alesina and Tabellini, 1987) (Backus and Drifill, 1985) (Barro, 1986).

Anticipating upon further developments in this area, one could advance already in an overly simplified way some insights drawn from reputation models. As investments in brand names reduce information costs for the private sector, so do investments in reputation by governments. A government's reputation will be determinant for its policy effectiveness and electoral success. Reputation enhances credibility and induces economic agents to adjust their behaviour, as they will perceive policy changes not merely as transitory, but reflecting a permanent course. Hence, reputation leaves also room for a "modified activist policy" as an alternative to a "rules policy". Reputation eventually will allow governments to engage in political cyclical behaviour, however, not unlimited. There is a trade-off, as it undermines its credibility and depreciates its brand name "reputation". One may wonder whether political business cycles may not be explained as corresponding to cycles in investment and depreciation of reputation?

4.3. Class conflicts and public choice

Within the already more established approach, the main theme of Dr. Borooah is the importance of group behaviour and conflicts in explaining political economics. The importance of class conflicts is emphasized in the discussion of popularity functions, i.e. the influence of economic variables on voting behaviour. It is also reiterated when looking into the policy reaction functions, analysing how governments are brought to manipulate economic events in order to secure an electoral advantage. Public choise theory is criticized for ignoring the differences in interests between the various groups in society.

In this respect criticism on popularity functions relying on the assumption of an homogeneous voter group may be warranted, but less so for the issue of policy-making. Public choice theory does not necessarily rely on the assumption of an homongenous society. Allowance is made for specialisation in the public sector by groups such as bureaucrats and politicians, but also by citizens into special interest groups that receive much attention in the literature. They are seen as using the political process in order to increase their share of national product, thereby often negatively affecting macro-economic policy-making. Class conflicts in particular are to be seen as a special case of polarization of the political process on distributional issues thereby leading to political instability.

Moreover, one may wonder whether in a society with a highly differentiated socioeconomic structure these groups conflicts are to be confined, as is suggested in the paper, to the old class distinction between capitalists and workers. Recent public choice literature points to the fact that the broad horizontal redistributions, such as between labour and capital, have been overtaken by more fragmented horizontal redistributions between a larger diversity of groups (Lindbeck, 1985) However, one must admit that these interrelationships between interest groups and their effect on policy-making remain still to be empirically explored (Mueller, 1987).

The same evidence on profits and wage shares, that is referred to in the paper to prove that the political business cycle is the result of class conflict between workers and capitalists, might also be explained by other hypotheses. These hypotheses should take into account that the labour share includes an increasing part of social security contributions and taxes, the proceeds of which are redistributed as transfer incomes to the non-active part of the population. The political business cycle would then be the result of a more complex three-way interaction between governments, labour and capital. Governments are not just manipulated by capitalists but play a more independent, but not very transparant role as redistributor towards various groups in society. In the process workers attempt to shift the higher tax burdens to the business sector, thereby eroding profits, investments and the productive base of the economy. A vicious circle process is started as the resulting higher unemployment has further repercussions leading in turn to higher expenditures; increasing tax burdens, less profits, less investments etc.

To summarize, macroeconomic policy-making is the outcome of social and economic forces, as stated in the paper, but is often the result of much more complex interactions. However, one may wonder whether the understanding of these interactions is the main issue to be clarified. Given the demand for interventions by various groups in society, is it not more important to know how the supply side of the political process interacts with these demands? Should our primary concern not to be to investigate how differences in political decision rules and institutions "filter" the same type of forces and conflicts quite differently? To what degree do the rules of the game as embodied in political institutions determine the outcome (Lindbeck, 1985)? This is also the question to be raised when moving into the next topic of the link between the rise of public expenditures and the organisation of the budgetary process.

4.4. Public expenditures and the organisation of the budgetary process

The specific contribution of the paper consists of a more detailed analysis of the rise in government expenditures in the U.K. over the past two decades.

Numbers on the evolution of general government expenditures, as well as percentages shares of GDP, should always be handled with caution, especially when converted in real terms. In the paper only the GDP deflator is used to deflate all types of government expenditures. When using several price deflators, e.g. an investment good price deflator for capital programmes, a price index of public consumption for government consumption and so on, the results may differ. For the U.K. such a weighted share of general government expenditures as a percentage of GDP would turn out to be larger after the mid-seventies than the numbers reported in the paper. This is in contrast to other European countries for which the weighting procedure with various deflators reduces the ratio to GDP. Moreover for the U.K. it turns out that the rise of public consumption would be smaller, and the rate of increase of the share of current transfers substantially higher (Todd, 1983). After these corrections the U.K. would certainly move up in the OECD ranking of countries with huge government sectors. However, it would not fundamentally affect Dr. Borooah's analysis of the budgetary process.

It is claimed in the paper that the public choice theory is unable to explain sufficiently the rise in government expenditures. Hence, one has to resort to other appraoches in particular by disaggregating expenditures and by focusing on conflicts between government departments. A more disaggregated appraoch certainly provides more information. A disaggregated view, however, is also taken in public choice theories that advance various partial explanations for the rise of government expenditures such as : government as a provider of public goods and eliminator of externalities, as redistributor of income, the activities of interest groups, bureaucrats, etc.

For true, as already mentioned, the interaction between interest groups and government growth still remains to be empirically explored in public choice theory. Whatsoever, the question arises again whether it is not more important to analyze how different political rules and mechanisms accomodate these group conflicts, instead of limiting the investigatin to interactions and conflicts among a few groups?

The investigation into the oganisation of the budgetary process in the paper appears to implicitly address the latter question. Also the digression into local finances goes in the same direction : in fact it points to the importance of political mechanisms. Moreover, contrary tot some claims made, the paper does not give an in-dept-explanation of how underlying societal conflicts between government departments explain the growth of government. Does the question why the Treasury preaches parsimony against the other expenditure prone departments not bring us back into public choice theory? In particular, the author points to a tendency to underestimate inflation rates in Britain. However, it would be of interest to learn what political mechanisms, what types of negotiation processes lead to such a downward bias. In Belgium the outcome of the process generally is an overestimation of the inflation rate, provoked by the high income elasticity of tax revenus and the non-indexing of tax rates. The recent policy change towards full indexation of tax rates, i.e. a change in the rules of the game, has already affected the organisation of the budgetary process towards more austerity in government expenditures.

The interesting discussion on the budgetary process may learn us that certain political mechanisms may work under certain circumstances to contain government growth. In particular "cash limits" - or even better disaggregated cash limits or budgetary envelopes under the heading of more freedom under lower ceilings - may impose on the public sector the same "cash constrained behaviour" as is typical for the private sector. Discipline would be further enhanced if also the responsibility for raising revenues would be decentralised e.g. towards local authorities. The Swiss experience with lower government growth may be the example.

According to the principal agent problem it is more difficult to monitor politic:ans in larger and centralised communities, and also fiscal illusion may be more important in such a setting (Myhrman, 1985). From recent OECD data it has been concluded that federal states tend to have substantially lower levels of taxes and government expenditures. In the last two decades the percentage rise of fiscal pressure in centralised states has been on average about the double of the increase in federal states (Moesen and Vanneste, 1987).

With respect to the use of cash limits in the budgetary process, the question arises whether cash limits should be upheld by more stringent rules or institutional mechanisms, or could be left more freely to a "modified activist policy" framework for governments. It brings us back to the previous discussion on credibility and reputation of governments. Hence, also this comment has come full circle. As to the questions raised by Dr. Borooah, the conclusion of this comment is that the room for governments to manipulate macoeconomic policies to their electoral advantages will very much depend on the political institutions as well as on the reputation they have established.

References

Alesina, A., G. Tabellini, Credibility and Politics, Invited paper to the European Economic Association Meetings, August, 1987.

Borooah V, G. Van der Ploeg, Political aspects of the economy, Cambridge University Press, Cambridge, 1983.

Backus, D., J. Drifill, Inflation and Reputation, American Economic Review, 1985, 550-538.

Barro, R., Recent developments in the theory of rules versus discretion, Economic Journal, 1986, 23-37.

Lindbeck, A., Redistribution Policy and the Expansion of the Public Sector, Journal of Public Economics, 1985, 309-328.

Mueller, D.C., The Growth of Government, I.M.F. Staff Papers, 1987, 115-149.

Todd, D., The growht of public expenditures in E.C. countries 1960-81, Some reflections, Economic Papers, E.C., n° 29, 1983.

Myhrman, J., Reflections on the Growth of Government, Journal of Public Economics, 1985, 275-285.

Moesen, W., J. Vanneste, Fiscale Hervorming en Budgettaire Herordening, Economisch en Sociaal Tijdschrift, 1987, 491-522.

PART THREE:
PUBLIC CHOICE AND PUBLIC INVESTMENT POLICY

5. THE MANAGERIAL ANALYSIS OF PUBLIC INFRASTRUCTURE INVESTMENT POLICIES

Alain Verbeke*

5.1. Introduction

The issue of investment processes whereby financial resources are allocated "à fonds perdus", has not yet received much serious attention in the management or economics literature. Allocating resources "à fonds perdus" implies that no actor is deemed directly responsible for the production activities (and their outputs), which result from investment decisions. In other words, neither the decision makers, nor the economic actors who will benefit from an investment must bear clear responsibilities for the actual outputs generated by the investment. The traditional literature on project evaluation, whether for private or public organizations, implicitly assumes that the results of a private investment analysis or social cost benefit analysis for a number of projects will guide the behaviour of decision makers because these decision makers would benefit themselves from choosing the "best" projects. In reality, of course, this is not the case if resources are allocated "à fonds perdus". If no one is a) directly rewarded for choosing the projects with, e.g., the highest expected profitability or net social benefits, or b) sanctioned for choosing projects with lower expected profitability or net social benefits, there is no reason to assume a priori that decision makers would actually

* senior research fellow with the Belgian national foundation for scientific research at the university of Antwerp (RUCA) and visiting senior research fellow at the university of Toronto. This paper was written when the author held a visiting appointment at Dalhousie University. The author is indebted to Prof. Dr. J. van den Broeck for critical comments on an earlier version of this paper.

Julien van den Broeck (ed.), Public Choice, 105-144.
© 1988 by Kluwer Academic Publishers and Association of Post-Keynesian Studies.

prefer the best ranked projects according to an investment analysis. Such a situation often characterizes national investments in public infrastructure, whereby a) government funds projects, without imposing any ex post performance requirements on the actors who will benefit from the investments and b) public policy makers themselves have no clear incentive to select the projects with the highest expected net social benefits.

A wide body of normative literature exists, which aims at providing policy-makers with analytical tools to assist them in performing "effective" investment decisions, i.e. decisions which are guided by the goal of maximizing social efficiency, see Little and Mirrlees (1959) Dasgupta et al. (1972), Mueller (1979), Sugden (1981), Pattanaik and Salle (1983).

It has often been recognized, however, that the use of tools such as cost-benefit analyses does not guarantee at all that social efficiency is actually pursued by policy makers. In other words, the mere execution of formal social cost-benefit analyses does not imply an effective investment process, i.e. the actual pursuit of social efficiency.

Birgegard (1975) has criticized the neglect of process aspects in the traditional literature on project evaluation. His empirical work on the evaluation of public projects in Kenya, Zambia and Tanzania, demonstrates the sometimes limited relevance of the traditional literature on project evaluation, because it doesn't relate sufficiently to practical decision problems and can be used as "window-dressing" : in this case a pseudo-scientific method is used to rationalize the execution of project that were already implicitly accepted by decision makers. Similar conclusions were reached by Imboden (1978) who assessed the use of cost-benefit analyses for public investment processes in developing countries : "the major decisions on alternatives are taken very early in the project planning cycle when the problems are identified and project ideas formulated". Whence, social cost-benefit analyses were used mainly to justify choices that had already been made. Moreover, the public choice literature suggests that public policy makers act out of self-interest. The work by Buchanan and Tullock (1962), Tullock (1965)

Niskanen (1975), Breton (1974), Mueller (1979) and others in the field, yields many examples of self-serving behaviour by both politicians and bureaucrats; hence, it is naive to expect that the mere introduction of an analytical tool in a decision process will generate effective investment decisions, whereby effectiveness refers to the actual pursuit of social efficiency. A simple example may illustrate this point : Schenker and Bunamo (1973) performed quantitative research on the relation between political influence from U.S. Congress members and the expenditures of the Army Corps of Engineers, which dominates the development and execution of infrastructure waterworks programs in the United States. It appeared that the Army Corps of Engineers' expenditures had a significant relation to political influence: "this would imply that waterworks programs are, in some sense, pork barrel legislation and helps explain the [ineffectiveness] of the cost-benefit technique as applied to project selection" (Schenker and Bunamo, 1973, p. 557).

In this paper, we shall develop a new framework that deals with the effectiveness issue of investment processes whereby resources are allocated "à fonds perdus". In the first two sections we shall discuss the concept of effectiveness, especially as regards its use in the context of public investment decisions.

In the four last sections, a new framework will be developed for the analysis of infrastructural investment policies. Examples demonstrating the practical relevance of this framework will be given, mainly based upon the author's own empirical research, see Verbeke (1986).

The theoretical framework consists of three models, each of which provides a different perspective on public infrastructure investment policies. The first model, which is the rational objectives model, builds upon the concept of effectiveness as defined in the next section. The second model, the structural ineffectiveness model, relaxes one of the two main premises upon which the first model is built. Finally, the third model, the commitment model, also relaxes the second premise made when developing and applying the rational objectives model.

Finally, we should mention that, throughout this paper, a "selective rationality"-approach is used, meaning that we do not start from the

premise of maximizing behavior by bureaucrats or politicians, see
Leibenstein (1976), (1982).

5.2. The issue of effectiveness of an investment process

In this paper effectiveness is given a "goal achievement' significance.
This approach suggests that 'the higher the degree of goal achievement,
the greater the organization's effectiveness'.

Three elements should be emphasized in this respect :

1) in many complex organizations a multitude of goals is actually
   pursued by the different individuals and organizational sub-units that
   function in the organization. Hence, it should be clear that the
   'goals' used by an analyst or consultant to assess the effectiveness
   of organizational decision making always result from a normative
   approach as to 'whose' goals are relevant as a criterion of
   effectiveness;

2) if the effectiveness is studied of strategic investment processes, the
   definition of goal achievement solely in terms of 'final outputs',
   e.g. realized profits or social benefits, should be avoided. Strategic
   decisions, per definition are taken in circumstances of 'partial
   ignorance, see Ansoff (1965). Hence the final outcomes of an
   investment decision, e.g. its profits, may be largely influenced by
   unpredictable changes in environmental parameters, which are not
   controlled by the decision makers in the investment process. Hence,
   the question arises whether or not the effectiveness of the
   investment process can be assessed without using the ultimate
   outcomes of the investment as the core variable for performing this
   assessment.

3) Apart from the problem of partial ignorance, which is characteristic for strategic decision processes, the use of 'final outputs' as a core variable for assessing effectiveness should also be avoided if decision makers in the resource allocation process cannot influence activities in the production process, i.e. those activities that are performed as a result of the investments. This problem is represented in figure 1.

Figure 1 : Resource allocation and the issue of effectiveness.

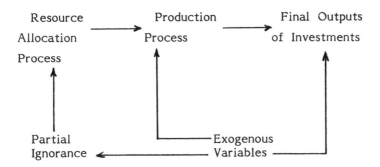

This figure highlights the problems faced by a policy analyst or consultant, when attempting to perform an assessment of the effectiveness of a resource allocation process. The final outputs of an investment can only be a good proxy for the effectiveness of the investment process if exogenous variables do not create high partial ignorance for the decision makers in the investment process and if the production process itself can be controlled by these same decision makers.

If this is not the case, the investment process should be assessed on its own, independently of the realized production process and realized final outputs. Is such an approach feasible and relevant, however?

Taking into account the three elements discussed above, this is only the case if the analyst or consultant is able to create standards against which the properties of allocative decision making can be compared. This requires a 'comparative institutional assessment", as explained in the next section.

5.3. The 'effectiveness' of public infrastructure investment policies.

In cases where public investments are not primarily meant to serve 'equity" objectives and choices have to be made among a large number of investment projects, the normative theory of welfare economics suggests that the projects with the highest benefit-cost ratios should be selected. Here, it is assumed that available resources are scarce and that projects are not mutually exclusive ; for a discussion of these issues and the rationale for the social cost-benefit approach, see Pearce and Nash (1980), Williams (1971).

An 'effective' investment process would then require that :

a)   a benefit-cost ratio is calculated for each project ;

b)   the projects are ranked in function of their benefit-cost ratio; and

c)   the projects with the highest benefit-cost ratio are selected for execution, given of course the problems of partial ignorance and absence of control of exogenous variables, which may largely influence the actual outcomes of the investments. It could then be argued that alternative methodological tools can be used, e.g. multicriteria analysis. In our view, the choice of a specific instrument to perform investment analyses is far less important than the answer to the question whether or not serious attempts are being made to evaluate the expected costs and benefits of the different projects in an objective way, and to select the 'best' projects, taking into account these costs and benefits. Effectiveness could then be defined as the development, evaluation, ranking and selection of investment projects so as to execute the best projects, whereby 'best' depends upon the costs and benefits associated with the different projects.

This approach only has practical relevance if two conditions can be fulfilled by the analyst or consultant.

Firstly, the analyst or consultant studying an investment process must be able to determine whether or not the goal mentioned above is actually pursued by public policy makers. Secondly, if ineffectiveness is observed, the analyst or consultant must be able to suggest 'alternative methods' of decision making, which would lead to a higher effectiveness and the implementation of which is feasible. In other words, it makes no sense to criticize the ineffectiveness of a present situation if this ineffectiveness is 'measured' against an ideal state of affairs which only exists in theory and is based on implausible behavioral premises.

If it is assumed that, in practice, effective and ineffective investment behavior can be distinguished and that ineffective behavior can be corrected, in principle, this has a specific implication ; it means that, as a result of a comparative institutional assessment, the consultant or analyst favours an alternative decision process, which can be implemented in practice at negligible monetary costs and would lead to a higher degree of goal achievement.

Transaction cost theory as developed by Williamson (1975) (1985) to analyze the internal functioning of large private corporations, provides a methodological tool to perform such a comparative institutional assessment. It can only be used, however, if two assumptions can be made. Firstly, one or a number of decision makers must exist who actually pursue the achievement of an effective decision making process as defined above. Secondly, these decision makers must be able to eliminate ineffective decision making, if observed.

Williamson's theory is based upon two behavioral premises : bounded rationality and opportunism. The former reflects the fact that economic actors are intendedly rational, but experience limits in formulating and solving complex problems and in processing (receiving, storing, retreiving, transmitting) information. The latter refers to self-interest seeking with guile. In organizations, opportunism may take the form of subgoal pursuit, whereby individuals identify and pursue 'local goals' at the possible expense of 'global goals', i.e. those goals that are used as parameters to assess effectiveness. Given these two behavioral premises, the assessment of the effectiveness of an investment process can be reduced to answering the question whether or not the existing decision structure, i.e. the way in which resource allocation activities are spread over different actors and then coordinated, economizes on bounded rationality and attenuates opportunism (both of which hinder organizational goal achievement) as compared with alternative decision structures.

Based upon the empirical research of Chandler (1962), Williamson has performed such an analysis to assess the effectiveness of different organizational structures, in terms of their properties to stimulate the pursuit of increasing shareholders' wealth. It then appeared that a functional structure (or U-form) in large corporations limited the ability of corporate managers to handle the volume and complexity of the demands placed upon them, while the functional parts of the organization (e.g. sales, engineering, production) engaged in subgoal pursuit (which was partly a manifestation of opportunism). The multidivisional structure (or M-form) appeared to be more 'effective' as it removes the corporate executives from becoming involved in day-to-day decisions and allows them to concentrate on strategic, long term issues. Moreover, it adds the possibility to use internal incentive and control instruments which allow the elimination of opportunistic behavior, especially subgoal pursuit.

A similar analysis can be made to assess the effectiveness of alternative decision structures in terms of their properties to stimulate the pursuit of social efficiency in resource allocation processes.
Such an analysis will be performed in the fourth section of this paper when developing the rational objectives model.

5.4. The Relevance of a Multiple Perspectives Appraoch for the Analysis of Infrastructural Investment Processes

If public resources are allocated "à fonds perdus" for the execution of national infrastructure projects, two initial starting points are possible. On the one hand, one can start from the premise that national goal such as the pursuit of social efficiency can be used as a criterion for the evaluation of the effectiveness of the resource allocation process. On the other hand, the opposite premise can be put forward : national goals do not exist or cannot be used for purposes of effectiveness assessment.

If the former starting point is chosen, two additional research alternatives exist. First, the premise can be put forward that observed ineffectiveness can be eliminated immediately by decision makers who pursue the national goals; in this case a rational objectives model is used by the researcher. Second, one could argue that observed ineffectiveness will only be eliminated if the existing power structure in the organization is altered, and this will only take place under specific circumstances : a structural ineffectiveness model is then used by the researcher.

The second starting point mentioned above does not accept the relevance of 'national' objectives for infrastructural works. This case starts from the premise that investment decisions are made merely as the result of specific preferences of 'relevant' actors. Relevant actors are all individuals or groups who can influence the outputs of the investment process. The driving force of the investment process is commitment emanating from relevant actors to the execution of particular projects; in this case, a 'commitment' model is used. If the three approaches mentioned above are applied sequentially to the analysis of an investment process, the results of the use of the last two models, can be fed back to the results obtained through the use of the first model. It should be emphasized that the rational objectives model is normative, the structural ineffectiveness model partly normative and partly descriptive and the commitment model descriptive. The whole theoretical framework is represented in Figure 2.

A crucial question as to the relevance of using three models for the analysis of one investment process, is whether these models are complements or substitutes. In the former case, each model would give a partial explanation for the observed resource allocation activities. In the latter case, the 'best' model should be chosen. It is the contention of this paper that in many cases it is impossible for the researcher to determine ex ante whether national infrastructure policy objectives have relevance for the assessment of investment processes and whether certain actors exclusively pursue these possible objectives : the use of alternative models may then undoubtedly contribute to richer insights into these complex processes (see Allison (1971), Linstone (1984), Thomas (1984)). Ex post, the model perceived as the best may then still be chosen.

5.5. The Rational Objectives Model

A variety of research has been performed with respect to the development of optimal resource allocation structures in complex organizations such as large private firms. Examples include : Bergh (1965), Bower (1970), Ackerman (1970), Carter (1971), Vancil and Lorange (1975), Van Cauwenbergh and Cool (1982), Vancil and Green (1981), Burgelman (1980), Caves (1980).

Based upon this research a normative model is developed, as outlined in Figure 3, which describes an effective investment structure for solving complex resource allocation problems with six characteristics. These characteristics determine the boundaries within which effectiveness assesments have to be made.

First, basic objectives of national policies for infrastructure (objectives of final impactees, i.e. the taxpayers), can be identified and used as a criterion to assess the effectiveness of the investment process. The choice of these objectives is obviously always a normative issue. They can be drawn from the welfare economics literature or from in-depth interviews with policy-makers and the analysis of major policy documents. If the objectives are too vague, it may be necessary to identify more detailed objectives for different sub-sectors. In Verbeke (1986), such objectives were identified for public investments in Belgian seaports (until 1986, all infrastructure works in Belgian seaports were subsidized "à fonds perdus" for 100%). These include : a) the social profitability of seaport investments should be assessed in a systematic and objective fashion; b) complementary projects for the different seaports should be integrated in a national investment plan; c) a national

Figure 2 : A Multiple Perspectives System for the Analysis of Infrastructural Investment Processes

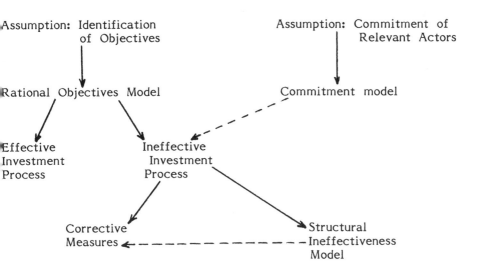

- - - - : Feedback of information generated through the use of one model
to the results obtained through the application of another model.

Figure 3 : Organizational Coordination and Control Mechanisms for
Investment Processes

Category Object	Cultural	Structural
Process		
Product		

investment plan should be created after consultation of all interested parties. The first element clearly refers to the basic objective from the normative literature on welfare economics, with which the policy makers seem to agree. The two latter elements should be interpreted as additional specifications of a decision structure fostering the realization of the former element. Through the use of such objectives, one of the three following statements can be made on any observed pattern of resource allocation activities : (a) the resource allocation activities are effective; (b) the resource allocation activities are ineffective; (c) no judgement can be made on the (in)effectiveness of the resource allocation activities.

Second, three categories of decision activities can be distinguished: strategic, administrative and operational activities. Strategic activities include the definition of basic investment objectives and the purpose of the investments, the determination of structural coordination and control mechanisms (see infra) and the development of investment projects. Strategic decisions, by definition, cannot be completely programmed, and are made in a situation of partial ignorance, see Ansoff (1965). Administrative or programmable decisions consist of the determination of the volume of resources available for allocation and the evaluation and selection of investment projects. Administrative decisions can always be programmed in principle. Finally, operational decisions include the authorization to invest funds and the control upon the actual use of the allocated resources.

Third, three levels of authority can be distinguished in the structure through which the resource allocation process flows: a strategic, an administrative and an operational level. The strategic level is supposed to exclusively pursue national policy objectives for infrastructure. This level would include the national ministry that is formally responsible for the pursuit of national infrastructure policies. In the case of Belgian sea port policy, this ministry is the Ministry of Transport. Parliament and the national government could also be regarded as segments of the strategic level, but their 'decision agenda' is supposed to include broader and more general objectives than those of infrastructural policy, so that they will often only act as 'sponsor' and be involved in authorization decisions. The administrative level is explicitly charged with performing 'administrative decision making activities'; in many countries special committees, agencies or ministries have been set up in order to perform investment analyses and other administrative tasks related to the evaluation and execution of infrastructural projects. In some cases, a distinction between strategic and administrative level will not be easy to make, as all national activities with respect to the handling of infrastructural investment projects may be concentrated in one ministry; mostly, there will be a clear distinction, however, between the actors responsible for national goal setting and the actors performing administrative activities. In the case of Belgian seaport policy, the administrative level consists of the Ministry of Public Works and the National Commission for Seaport Policy. Is should be emphasized that the strategic as well as the administrative level may consist of politicians and bureaucrats. It is our contention that investment preferences of different politicians or bureaucrats may completely diverge and do not necessarily always relate to vote - or budget maximizing considerations, see Jackson (1983). In the case of Belgian sea port policy, regional preferences of both bureaucrats and politicians for the allocation of public funds were often observed. Moreover, we also observed that a department (bureaucracy) may primarily serve the minister (politician) and promote his policies, so that each ministry (including the minister and his department) may act as a sovereign power. Finally, the operational level performs or controls production activities that will take place as a result of the investments. In the case of infrastructure such as roads, a distinct operational level may not exist, and investment proposals may originate from a large and diffuse set of actors, including building contractors, regional development agencies, or other clientele groups. In the case of a seaport sector, the operational level consists primarily of the seaport authorities themselves. With respect to these three levels, it should be emphasized that certain administrative activities may also be carried out by the strategic or the operational level, while the administrative level may engage in certain strategic and operational activities.

Fourth, the administrative and the operational level possess discretionary power, in the spirit of Tullock (1965), Lindsay (1976), Brown and Jackson (1982), Jackson (1983). Both may be driven by local goals, i.e., by objectives which conflict with the national objectives for infrastructural investments. If investment projects generated by the operational level are developed in function of subgoal pursuit, they are called autonomous projects. This problem is especially acute for infrastructure investments whereby projects can be generated by any interested economic actor, who may then try to form a 'coalition' with the administrative level, in order to secure funds for the execution of this project. In Belgian seaport policy such coalitions have been observed between the ministry of public works and different segments of the operational level.

Fifth, the strategic level does not exert control on the production activities that are performed as a result of the outcomes of the investment process, nor does it exert cultural controls (as defined by Baliga and Jaeger (1984)), on the investment process. In Figure 3, the different possible organizational coordination and control mechanisms that can be used in a resource allocation process are represented, see also Child (1973), Ouchi (1977, Mintzberg (1979). The object of coordination and control can obviously only be the actual resource allocation processes, i.e., the decision activities that are performed, or the outputs of the resource allocation process, i.e., the investment plans and/or budgets. Activities as well as outputs can only be coordinated and controlled in two ways, namely through cultural and structural systems. Cultural or informal mechanisms generate shared patterns of objectives and beliefs as to what constitutes effective resource allocation behaviour and outputs. This paper will only be concerned with organizations restricted to structural systems. Such a restriction will often hold in the public sector where it may be extremely difficult, if not impossible to generate a shared frame of reference among all actors involved, on the importance and necessity to pursue national goals through informal systems.

Sixth, the strategic level has two instruments at its disposal to eliminate subgoal pursuit. In the first place, it can determine the inancial volume available for allocation. In the second place it can nfluence the coordination and control systems in the investment process, uch as institutionalized a) division and integration of decision activities; •) reward and sanction systems related to the resource allocation process; ind c) limiting conditions with reference to the nature and the scope of nvestment projects, which will be considered for execution.

Assuming that an investment problem is characterized by the •lements mentioned above, the question arises, what will be the impact •f changes in the structural coordination and control systems ? Influencing hem may result in a reduction of subgoal pursuit and autonomous nvestment projects. Changes in these structural systems may generate the ievelopment of so called induced investment projects and decision making ictivities, which are in line with the national objectives for nfrastructural investments.

The problem is that the strategic level cannot continuously exert a •erfect control upon the activities of the actors who develop investment •rojects (operational level or outside actors). However, choices need to be nade between the proposed projects. Hence, a confrontation between the •asic objectives of the organization and the investment projects coming rom the operational level or outside actors is required. A distinction .hould be made between confrontations related to strategic matters (could he investment project fit in a national investment plan?) and :onfrontations concerning administrative matters (is the investment project •rofitable?). In the presence of subgoal pursuit, these confrontations should •bviously be institutionalized as a major structural control system. In the :ase of Belgian seaport policy, such confrontations are supposed to take •lace in the National Commission for Seaport Policy. It should be •mphasized that the possibility to influence the investment process hrough the formal decisions to allocate resources (authorization stage) is •ery limited, since these decisions are mostly taken under high :omparative ignorance as defined by Mintzberg et al. (1976).

If an investment problem is characterized by the six elements nentioned above, a normative model of strategic resource allocation ictivities can be constructed, as described in Figure 4, and which can be given a comparative institutional interpretation.

5.6. A Comparative Institutional Interpretation of Figure 4

First, the existence of bounded rationality, which is defined as the limited capacity of the human mind for formulating and solving complex problems, compared with the size of problems whose solution is required for objectively rational behaviour in the real world, see Simon (1957) and Williamson (1975). This principle of bounded rationality has two effects on the investment process.

a) Realistic investment projects can only be generated by the operational level or outside actors who are familiar with the complexity and instability of the environment in which "production activities" take place.

b) The effective assessment and administrative handling of investment projects requires the introduction of specialized staff at the administrative level, who have the technical ability to perform administrative activities.

Second, given the fact that the administrative and operational level dispose of discretionary power in the investment process, the problem of opportunism arises, i.e. 'the incomplete or distorted disclosure of information, especially to calculated efforts to mislead, distort, disguise obfuscate or otherwise confuse. It is responsible for real or contrived conditions of information asymmetry' (Williamson, 1985, p. 47). This problem of opportunism arises in the first place when certain actors guided by subgoals, try to carry through autonomous investment projects.

Since a continuous direct control of the activities of the operational level or outside actors would be too costly or in some cases unfeasible, selective screening mechanisms have to be introduced as structural coordination and control systems, making a so called strategic and administrative confrontation possible, in order to eliminate the projects that do not fit in a national investment plan. These confrontation activities should not be regarded as the result of mechanistic arrangements but may be dependent upon the skill in advocacy and political weight' of the actors concerned. For example, if the strategic confrontation is activated at the administrative level, members of this level may have to perform the difficult task of providing impetus to certain projects (convincing the strategic level that these projects should be executed) and demanding an adaptation or elimination of others.

The model represented in Figure 4 thus provides an effective governance structure that allows the pursuit of social efficiency in cases where the investment problem has the six characteristics we described above.; through the implementation of this model a complex organization can economize on bounded rationality, while simultaneously safeguarding the investment process against the hazards of local rationality and opportunism as compared with situations whereby, e.g. no elements are introduced in the structural context to eliminate subgoal pursuit or whereby the strategic level would attempt to centralize strategic decision making, hence exacerbating the problem of bounded rationality. It should be emphasized that this model is somewhat different from Williamson's (1975, 1985) M-structure. Several empirical studies have shown that resource allocation structures in complex organizations, require a spread of strategic decision activities over different organizational levels and not a concentration at the highest level, as Williamson would suggest, see Bower (1970), Burgelman (1980), McGuiness and Conway (1986).

As an example, we shall now apply this normative model to infrastructural investments in Belgian seaports. It has been shown in Verbeke (1986) that the resource allocation problem national policy-makers are confronted with, when subsidizing infrastructural and superstructural works in Belgian seaports, is indeed characterized by the six elements which we already mentioned. Hence, the design of an effective governance structure for allocating national resources can be regarded as a comparative institutional problem, which requires a structure as described above.

a. The problem of bounded rationality

The local seaport authorities (operational level) and private port users are the only actors who can generate meaningful public investment proposals to build infrastructural works, since they possess crucial information concerning, e.g., competition in the Le Havre-Hamburg range. Moreover, the technical assessment and administrative handling of investment projects at the national level can only be performed by specialized public officials. It is the administration of the ministry of public works (administrative level) which is responsible for performing administrative activities. All public funds for seaport investments are allocated through the budget of the ministry of public works. Local sections of this ministry maintain close contacts with the seaport authorities and collect their investment proposals. The ministry of public works is ever represented in the board of directors of the seaports of Zeebrugge and Brussels.

b. The problem of opportunism (subgoal pursuit)

Neither the seaport authorities nor the ministry of public works seem interested in the pursuit of the three national objectives of seaport policy. Therefore, the problem of opportunism is an important issue. Seaport authorities enjoy an almost complete discretion when generating investment projects and are mainly interested in the allocation of sufficient public resources to execute all their projects, with as little national controls as possible. When national budgetary limitations do not allow the execution of all projects, each seaport authority pursues two objectives. First, to obtain a maximum amount of resources within the given zero-sum situation. Second, to decide as autonomously as possible on the investment priorities, given the obtained amount of resources. The activities of the ministry of public works also seem to be dominated by subgoal pursuit for three main reasons. First, its engineers are often involved in the technical development of investment projects, even at early stages of their development, so that in many cases commitment is built up to execute these projects. Second, the ministry of public works pursues an active policy in favour of certain segments of the construction

Figure 4

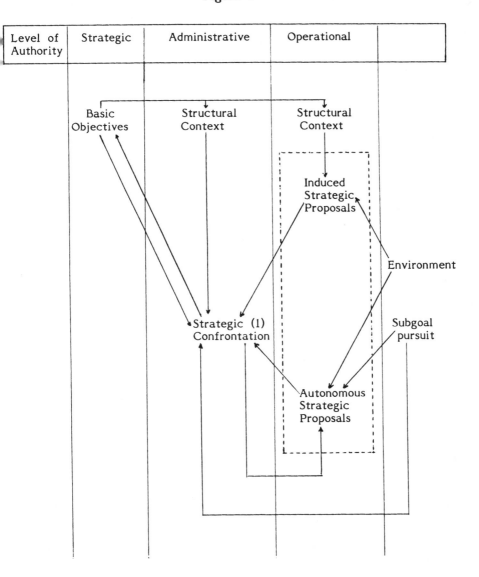

(1) In this figure it is assumed that the strategic confrontation takes place at the administrative level on principle such a confrontation can also take place at the strategic level.

sector, especially large specialized building contractors. Hence seaport investment proposals are often regarded as a means for the survival of large construction firms. This objective should not necessarily be in contradiction with national seaport policy objectives, but it explains why the attention of the ministry of public works is often directed towards the execution of projects rather than towards their economic evaluation. Third, the promotion and reward structure for civil engineers of the ministry of public works is partly based on the volume and complexity of the works designed and executed.

The question then arises whether the necessary bureaucratic controls have been introduced to eliminate the impact of subgoal pursuit on the outcomes of the investment process.

A low cost selective screening mechanism has indeed been set up by the minister of transport in the form of a national commission for seaport policy, established in 1978. The composition of the commission includes, among others, representatives of the ministries of transport and public works and the seaport authorities so that it cannot be expected to exclusively pursue national interests. The commission was not only charged with performing strategic activities (e.g., prescribing the specific tasks that each seaport should perform, based on an economic analysis of their competitive strengths and weaknesses) but also with administrative tasks (e.g., assessing the social profitability of each project). Hence, the commission can be regarded as a part of the administrative level in seaport policy.

Finally, it should be noted that the advice of the commission, with respect the execution of investment projects is not obligatory, but only optional. The main question then arises whether this commission has been able to generate serious strategic and administrative confrontations aimed at eliminating the impact of subgoal pursuit.

On the basis of an extensive empirical analysis, two conclusions were drawn that indicated the ineffectiveness of Belgian seaport policy.

First, the strategic level, and more precisely the ministry of transport, does not exert any influence on the strategic activities of the ministry of public works and the seaport authorities. Second, the national commission for seaport policy has been unable to generate a strategic and administrative confrontation for which it was set up because it lacks logistic support from the ministry of transport.

Moreover, the seaport authorities and the ministry of public works presently dominate the activities of the commission and provide all its basic inputs. The administrative activities of the commission are restricted to a confrontation between subgoal pursuit by the seaport authorities and the subgoal pursuit by the ministry of public works. It should be considered as a 'post factum' confrontation, since the administrative programs of the ministry of public works which are discussed in the commission are themselves the result of a complex bargaining process with the different seaport authorities.

We proposed a number of changes in order to generate a more effective governance structure. First, an extension of the competencies of the national commission for seaport policy is required, through a greater involvement of the ministry of transport, especially in the area of strategic decision making. Moreover, the ministry of transport should provide logistic support to the commission, e.g., through establishing a specialized staff of economists and engineers who would perform uniform social cost-benefit analyses for all large projects and macroeconomic studies of the demand for seaport infrastructural works. These studies should then be used as inputs for the strategic and administrative confrontation and compared with projects coming from the seaport authorities and the ministry of public works. Second, the composition of the national commission for seaport policy should be restricted to actors who do not gain direct 'advantages' from the execution of specific investment projects. Hence, the ministry of public works and the seaport authorities should be excluded from the commission. They should only be allowed to present and defend their projects before the commission, which should then autonomously assess whether these projects could fit into a national investment plan, based upon the economic complementarity of the different seaports, using portfolio analysis techniques to assess the comparative advantages of every seaport for different traffic types (strategic activity). It should also evaluate the social profitability of projects, in a systematic fashion (administrative activity).

The two changes mentioned above are in accordance with the principles of organizational design as set forth by Simon (1973), whereby the total set of decision activities that needs to be performed is distributed among relatively independent subsystems, each one of which can be designed with only minimal concern for its interaction with the others. The benefits of Simon's organization design are that, in this case activities of the national commission would be clearly separated from the activities performed by agents persuing subgoals. Whence, the commission should have the same function as the board of directors in a private corporation, which is to protect the interests of the shareholders. In this case, the commission's function would be to safeguard the use of the nations resources which face a significant risk of opportunistic behaviour, since no actor is deemed directly and totally responsible for the results of the use of the resources involved.

The case of Belgian seaport policy was only one example in which the rational objectives model could be used as a prescriptive policy instrument to assess and possibly eliminate ineffectiveness in infrastructural investment policies. The main idea behind the model is that investment projects for national infrastructure often are not generated in function of national objectives; Hence, not the budget decisions (operational activities) are crucial, but the choice of investment projects and their integration in a national investment plan.

Finally, we should mention that alternative decision structures for conducting Belgian seaport policy may also lead to a higher effectiveness. This would be a situation of 'equifinality' whereby different means may lead to a similar degree of goal achievement. The main purpose of our analysis was, however, to demonstrate that substituting a new decision structure for an old one may lead to the elimination of ineffective decision making if the new structure allows to ameliorate the problem caused by bounded rationality and opportunism.

5.7. The Structural Ineffectiveness Model

The rational objectives model described in the previous section has two important limitations.

First, the assumed existence of a strategic level, which would exclusively pursue national infrastructural objectives may be questioned. The actors who are assumed to defend the interests of the national community may well agree upon the existence of national policy objectives but their actual behaviour can completely deviate from this. In this case a 'sub-strategic' level also partly guided by subgoal pursuit, substitutes for the strategic level. This is a basis premise of public choice theory, see Downs (1967) and Buchanan (1984), which is also sometimes put forward by detractors of the use of social cost-benefit analyses, see Stewart (1978). Arnold (1981), following Maass (1951), observed that infrastructural works in U.S. ports result from ineffective decisions of Congress (sub-strategic level), since the individual members of Congress would also pursue local objectives, and all projects are placed in a so called 'omnibus bill', thus providing the ideal circumstances for logrolling. The Army Corps of Engineers (administrative level) performs technical and economic analyses, including cost-benefit analyses; it is remarkable that this adminisitrative level has the tendency to systematically overestimate the benefits of certain projects and underestimate their costs. Such an ineffective policy can be maintained because most projects generate concentrated costs for specific interest groups and members of Congress, while the costs are spread over all tax payers, in the spirit of Olson (1965).

Second, the rational objectives model does not explain the existence of ineffectiveness in decision processes. If ineffectiveness could immediately be eliminated, why then is the negative impact of bounded rationality and opportunistic behaviour not continuously reduced through changes in the structural coordination and control mechanisms?

The rational objectives model implicitly assumes that the strategic level pursues the achievement of social efficiency through the investment process, given the information available to it, i.e., within the constraints created by the problem of bounded rationality in the organization. If a consultant or analyst perceives ineffectiveness, in the sense that an alternative organizational structure would be more appropriate for the pursuit of social efficiency, additional information is given to the strategic level; this should then lead to an elimination of ineffectiveness. In other words, the existence of ineffectiveness is itself a direct result of bounded rationality from the part of the strategic level, a problem which can be overcome through information provided by the policy analyst or consultant. In contrast, the structural ineffectiveness model is based upon the cynical view that public investments are prirmarily based upon the self-intrest of powerful individuals and groups involved in the resource allocation process, although most, if not all of these actors would agree that, in principle, social efficiency should be pursued. This situation is similar to the case of managers in private business firms who agree that the pursuit of shareholder's wealth should be the prime objective of the firm, but who, in reality, engage in discretionary behaviour and may pursue goals which conflict with the shareholders' goals, see, e.g., Berle and Means (1932), Baumol (1959), Marris (1946), Williamson (1964), Galbraith (1967).

The structural ineffectiveness model starts from the premise that monetary costs necessitated to influence the structural coordination and control systems and to generate a higher effectiveness are negligible, and yet this context may only be changed in exceptional circumstances. This does obviously not imply that no coordination and control costs exist in the organization, but only that a) different organizational structures are associated with different levels of coordination and control costs and b) the introduction of a new structure can often be introduced at negligible monetary costs. If no such new organizational structure is introduced although it would allow to limit subgoal pursuit and it would ameliorate the problem of bounded rationality, this paradoxal situation is defined as inertia, i.e. the non-elimination of observed ineffectiveness although this elimination could be performed at negligible monetary costs. The concept of inertia is explained in depth in Verbeke (1986). The prime sources of inertia are described in Figure 5.

The reason why the sub-strategic level would not alter the structural coordination and control systems, even when it would have a preference for the elimination of subgoal pursuit by the administrative and/or operational level is that attempts to change the power structure as it exists on a specific point in time may endanger the power position of the sub-strategic level itself.

Every attempt to eliminate ineffectiveness, causes a destabilization of existing decision patterns and a change in the discretionary power that one or more (sub) levels in the hierarchy of an organizaton enjoy on a specific point in time, i.e. in a static perspective, with a given structural context.

In a dynamic perspective, the structural context can be changed by the sub-strategic level, but resistance to change may be expected as static power positions will be touched; the problem here is the lack of predictability with respect to the reactions of affected subsystems in the organization. The stronger this lack of predictability, the less changes in the structural context can be expected.

The distribution of power in the resource allocation process is dependent upon five elements. First, the authority of higher hierarchical levels to determine the structural context at lower levels; secondly, information and coordination costs which make impossible a continuous control and correction of activities of lower hierarchical levels. These two sources of power were already implicitly recognized when developing the rational objectives model, the latter element clearly puts boundaries on the possibilities to eliminate subgoal pursuit and economize on bounded rationality. Thirdly, the centrality of decision activities performed by the different subsystems in the organization, depending upon the interdependencies with other subsystems in the organization (quantity and intensity of interaction), see, Pennings et al. (1969, p. 427). Fourthly, the non-substitutability of decision activities performed by the different subsystems in the organization, i.e. the difficulty of having these activities performed by other actors. Fifthly, the coping with uncertainty by the different subsystems in the organization, namely through providing predictability to the development and the outcomes of the decision

Figure 5 : Sources of inertia

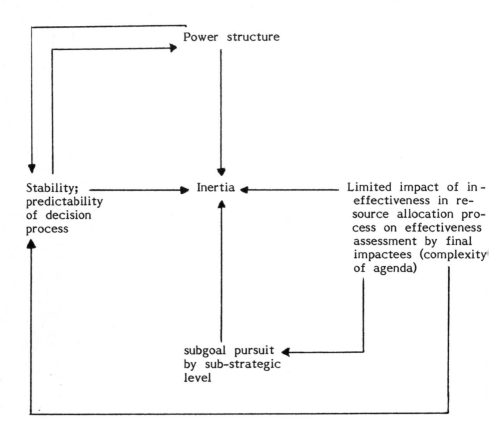

process. The importance of coping with uncertainty in organizations was recognized by Thompson (1967) who developed an organizational theory with uncertainty as its central subject.

The three latter sources of power can potentially be altered by using the first source of power, since coping with uncertainty, as well as non-substitutability and centrality of decision activities depend on the structural context.

The reason why the sub-strategic level would not alter the structural context, even when it would prefer to eliminate subgoal pursuit of the administrative and/or operational level (or subsystems herein) is that attempts to change the existing (static) power structure may endanger the (static) power position of the sub-strategic level itself, precisely because of the lack of predictability of the reactions of the affected subsystems.

A second and related explanation for inertia is the assumed preference for stability and uncertainty reduction of the different actors involved in the investment process, see, e.g. Thompson (1967). This idea is similar to the concept of 'ratchet rationality' (Leibenstein, 1976). See also Earl (1984). This issue cannot simply be reduced to a problem of subgoal pursuit by the sub-strategic level, nor is it merely an expression of bounded rationality. It refers to what decision theorists have termed bootstrapping, i.e. reliance on codified experience : once a problem is identified, an existing solution to a similar problem is applied to it. Such behavior may easily lead to inertia. It can "...produce erroneous judgements; furthermore the ease with which they are applied inhibits the search for superior methods", see Fischhoff, Slovic, Lichtenstein and Keeney (1981, p. 28), see also Jones and Thompson (1984).

If the observed ineffectiveness only has a minor impact upon the effectiveness assessment by the final impactees (voters, taxpayers), inertia may be maintained and the existing stability of the decision making processes increased. The reason no intervention is generated by the final impactees thus essentially follows from the complexity of their agendas. For a discussion of this concept, see Loasby (1976). Given a situation whereby ineffectiveness is not eliminated by the sub-strategic level, as a result of a) subgoal pursuit by the sub-strategic level; b) its preference for stability; c) the existing power structure in the organization; and/or d) the complexity of the final impactees' agendas, the question should be answered under which circumstances ineffectiveness could be reduced.

Three possibilities should be considered : First, a 'delegation' of decision power to a so called higher authority, e.g., a consultancy bureau or a supra-national organization. The concept of 'higher authority' refers to actors who form part, neither of the final impactees nor of the sub-strategic, the administrative or the operational level, but whose objectives converge with the objectives of the final impactees (e.g., when a consultant is hired to act as a change-agent). Second, an elimination of ineffectiveness resulting from the perception of exogenous pressure (coming from the environment) or bad results as perceived by the sub-strategic level. Changes in exogenous pressure refer to changes in the 'sanctions' that will accompany the non-elimination of ineffectiveness (e.g., a loss of votes). Third, 'internal control', resulting from exogenous pressure or unsatisfactory results of the production activities may also reduce ineffectiveness. Internal control means that actors involved in the resource allocation process exert control upon each other and/or upon the sub-strategic level, in order to bring the investment process in line with national infrastructural objectives. The reason for this internal control lies in the recognition, from the part of the actors involved, that the existing ineffective resource allocation processes are nog favourable to them and that procedures conforming with national infrastructure objectives would be preferable, compare with Crew et al. (1971) and McCain (1975).

Internal control thus may have two consequences. First, the creation of a costless information system, which reduces what we called the boundary (minimal) level of coordination and control costs and thus strengthens the relative power position of the sub-strategic level without changes in structural coordination and control systems. Second, the generation of pressure on the sub-strategic level to eliminate structural ineffectiveness, so that the preference for the pursuit of own objectives and for stability from the part of this level may be overcome and the structural coordination and control system altered.

The application of the structural ineffectiveness model to infrastructural investments in Belgian seaports led to an interesting interpretation of many decision activities. First, it appeared that the ministry of public works and the seaport authorities actually dominate resource allocation activities, because their respective power positions are extremely important. Second, it was observed that the national commission for seaport policy was not set up as a low cost screening mechanism at all. The national commission was established in 1978, because the Minister of Transport has been urged by members of parliament (guided by regional considerations) and representatives of the port of Antwerp to express his position on port policy (the expansion of the port of Zeebrugge has stirred up animosity coming from the port of Antwerp). The Minister of Transport, who lacked all competence in the field of port policy, then set up the national commission, partly because of voting considerations. It was intended to serve as a lightning conductor : if all parties represented in the commission could come to an agreement, the Ministry of Transport would be able to adopt the conclusions of the commission. If no consensus could be reached in the commission, the Ministry of Transport would not be bound to take a clear position; hence, the commission was only set up as result of 'internal control' exerted by actors unsatisfied with the existing investment policy. Moreover, it was observed that neither parliament nor the national governement as a whole have any serious interest in the pursuit of national seaport policy objectives; the situation cannot be explained by the complexity of their agendas (pursuit of broader macroeconomic policy goals), but by their preference not to disrupt existing decision patterns. Hence, a major source of ineffectiveness becomes clear : the actors who should pursue the basic objectives of seaport policy have little or no impact in the actual decision making process, and are not interested at all in the pursuit of national investment goals. A similar conclusion holds for the authorization decisions performed by the national government and parliament. Whence, only if, for example, exogenous pressure would become very high, possibly as a result of budgetary restrictions, it can be expected that additional formal power would be granted to the national commission for seaport policy. Even if its power were extended and the Ministry of Public Works and the seaport authorities excluded from its structure, it should be remembered that none of the remaining members of the commission can be expected te exclusively pursue national policy objectives; they may well be mixed motives bureaucrats, combining self-interest and the pursuit of national policies (Downs, 1967). In other words, social efficiency would only be pursued if pressure, such as exogenously determined limits on budget size would force the sub-strategic level to actually assess all projects in an objective way and to choose the 'best' projects, in order to make its decisions acceptable in the eyes of the actors who have overlapping claims on the available scarce resources.

The Commitment Model

The two models outlined in the previous sections have an important limitation.

Neither the rational **objectives** model, nor the structural ineffectiveness model can be **used** to analyze and assess decision processes that take place in an organized anarchy as defined by Cohen et al. (1972, p. 7) : "A theory of organized anarchy will describe a portion of almost any organizations's activities, but will not describe all of them".

Such a situation can be described by three elements. First, objectives that could be used as a guideline when assessing the effectiveness of resource allocation processes do not exist, see Perrow (1961, p. 855), Weick (1979, p. 101) and Mintzberg (1983, p. 240)

This problem is especially acute when final impactees consist of a heterogeneous set of actors without clearly converging objectives. Second, the existing decision processes are neither perfectly controlled, nor completely understood by the members involved in the decision making process, see Mintzberg and McHugh (1985). Third, the different levels as described in the first two models cannot be precisely determined and are very 'fluid'.

The commitment-model recognizes the difference between strategic, administrative and operational decisions, but mainly focuses on the commitment th at is built up from the moment on the idea for an investment project is created. The issue of 'commitment' is well developed in the management literature, see Aharoni (1966), Staw (1981), Schwenk (1984), Earl (1984).

To an extent, this model is closest to the public choice theory. Public investments in infrastructure are the result of transactions in the political market. Peltzman (1976, p. 747) viewed this market as follows: "The essential commodity being transacted in the political market is a transfer of wealth, with constituents on the demand side and their political representatives on the supply side".

In our view, this approach implies that ineffectiveness does not exist and that each existing decision pattern is 'optimal'.

The application of the commitment-model on infrastructural investment projects in Belgian seaports, led to conclusions that were completely different from those, reached through the use of the two other models. First, the existence of national policy objectives was rejected, as no actor in the resource allocation processes actually pursues these objectives on a permanent basis. Second, it appeared that most investment projects developed by the seaport authorities and other parties such as port users were a response to a complex set of exogenous stimuli upon which little or no control could be exerted. Hence, these investment projects could not merely be regarded as 'tools' through which 'subgoals' are pursued. Third, the relevance of structural coordination and control mechanisms was rejected since public policy makers involved in seaport policy are not elected, appointed or rewarded for the pursuit of national infrastructural objectives. The existing structure of property rights is not conducive to the pursuit of alleged national objectives. Moreover, no legitimate selectivity exists; legitimate selectivity would imply that the choice of investment projects by a particular actor (as the Minister of Transport) is accepted by all other actors involved in the resource allocation process; in reality, this is not the case. Unless all projects presented by the different seaport authorities are executed simultaneously, no consensus is possible on an optimal allocation of public resources. A decision taken at the national level, not to execute a project is mostly not perceived as a definitive decision by the actors promoting this project but merely as a delaying action. The concept of commitment was successfully used to describe and explain how investment projects are developed and pass through successive stages in the resource allocation process. This simple model, which is described in Verbeke (1986) allowed to contrast the diverging ways in which commitment is built up in the ports of Antwerp and Zeebrugge. In Antwerp, the private port users and the municipal port authority appeared to be the main actors initiating and developing investment projects. In Zeebrugge, it is the Ministry of Public Works and private building contractors who have generated most of the investment projects presently executed in this seaport. We demonstrated that the presence of bureaucrats from the Ministry of Public Works in the board of directors of the port of Zeebrugge and the incentive systems faced by these bureaucrats for executing large and sophisticated infrastructural works, largely contributed to the creation of commitment at the national level in order to develop this seaport after 1970.

Conclusions

The introducton to a managerial analysis of public infrastructure investment policies, presented in this article, started from the idea that it is often unclear whether a) national investment objectives can be used as an effectiveness criterion to assess investment policies and b) certain actors exclusively pursue these objectives.

The results of the application of the different models are obviously contradictory, but they make it possible to interpret observed resource allocation behaviour from different viewpoints, hence indicating that the identification and elimination of 'ineffectiveness' is an extremely complex issue.

We did not use a maximization approach, but a 'selective rationality' approach : the investment behaviour of politicians and bureaucrats with respect to infrastructure issues, which certainly does not always fit the pursuit of national objectives, is not necessarily always guided by vote- or budget maximization either. Only through process research can complex investment behaviour be described, analyzed and assessed. It is our contention that a multiple perspectives approach then provides a useful framework to perform such research. The case study of Belgian seaport investments was repeatedly referred to as an application of each of the three models. In Verbeke (1986), we concluded that the structural ineffectiveness model was the most appropriate to assess Belgian seaport policy, as no actor involved in the infrastructural investment processes actually pursues national objectives. On the other hand, we adopted the normative point of view, that national resources should only be allocated 'à fonds perdus' if national objectives are pursued. Hence, the present pork barrel policies were rejected, but we remained sceptical about the possibilities to implement an alternative decision structure: only under conditions of high 'exogenous pressure' or 'bad results' can such changes be expected. We should emphasize, however, that some experts on Belgian seaport policy, who were confronted with our work chose one of the two other models as the most appropriate. One academic preferred the first model, as he was convinced that statesmanship and political courage of the minister of transport would, in the long-run, lead to a change in the present resource allocation processes, which, he agreed, are now ineffective. Another expert, who had been involved in lobbying activities for the construction of the port of Zeebrugge argued that only the third model was relevant : "no one is interested in the pursuit of social efficiency. We were the most 'effective' ones in lobbying for money, and we got it".

Finally, the question should be asked, whether or not it is possible to eliminate the 'à fonds perdus' character of public infrastructure investment projects, in order to stimulate the pursuit of social efficiency. Such a measure was taken in October 1986 by the Belgian Government, which was faced with the macro-economic necessity to engage in budgetary cuts. The national government decided to decrease the national subsidization percentage for infrastructural works from 100 to 60%, in order to force local port authorities and port users to be more selective when developing investment projects and proposing the inexecution. In terms of the rational objectives model, this measure could be interpreted as a result of statesmanship and the will to eliminate ineffectiveness in resource allocation, as the non-subsidized part of investments would require at least some profitability. In terms of the structural ineffectiveness model, the national government took this decision, merely to avoid having to choose investment projects itself, as this would have resulted in strong reactions from the 'loosers", i.e. those actors whose projects would have been rejected. During the period 1976-1986 such criticism had been exerted by 'defenders' of the ports of Antwerp and Ghent. The introduction of the new subsidization system would reduce such behavior as the seaports would now be faced with the same necessity to find additional sources of funds when proposing a project and would not be able to criticize the 'ad hoc' nature of resource allocations as in the past. To an extent this measure was also an indirect result of 'internal control' by the proponents of the expansion of the Antwerp seaport, who were unsatisfied with the distribution of national resources among the different seaports and who were convinced that the port of Antwerp would receive a larger part of the available resources if the existing system of complete arbitrariness in the allocation of resources was replaced by a more 'objective' system, e.g., through the formal introduction of (a) social cost benefit analyses as a technique for project evaluation and selection and (b) 'market-powered incentives', whereby local port authorities and port users would have to come up with part of the required resources.

Finally, the commitment-model would explain this measure, by arguing that the commitment created at the national level for the execution of non-seaport investments had increased; hence the relative commitment to execute investments in seaport-infrastructure had declined. Thus, the decision to reduce the subsidization percentage had primarily a symbolic value, indicating that the focus of public infrastructure investments would partly shift away from seaport works toward other investment types.

References

Ackerman, R.W., Influence of Integration and Diversity on the Investment process, in Administrative Science Quarterly, Vol. 15, September 1970.

Aharoni, Y., The Foreign Investment Decision Process, Division of Research, Harvard Business School, Boston, 1966.

Allison, G.T., Essence of Decision: Explaining the Cuban Missile Crisis, Little Brown, Boston, 1971.

Ansoff, H.I., Corporate Strategy, An Analytic Approach to Business Policy for Growth and Expansion, McGraw-Hill, New York, 1965.

Arnold, R.D., Legislators, Bureaucrats and Locational Decisions, in Public Choice, Vol. 37, 1981.

Baliga, B. and Jaeger, A., Multinational Corporations: Control Systems and Delegation Issues, in Journal of International Business Studies, Vol. 15, No. 2, 1984.

Baumol, W.J., Business Behavior, Value and Growth, MacMillan, New York, 1959.

Berg, N., Strategic Planning in Conglomerate Companies, in Harvard Business Review, Vol. 43, No. 3, 1965.

Berle, A.A. and G.C. Means, The Modern Corporation and Private Property, Macmillan, New York, 1932.

Birgegard, L.E., The Project Selection Process in Developing Countries, A Study on the Public Investment Project Selection Process in Kenya, Zambia and Tanzania, Economic Research Institute, Stockholm School of Economics, Stockholm, 1975.

Bower, J., Managing the Resource Allocation Process: A Study of Corporate Planning and Investment, Division of Research, Graduate School of Business Administration, Harvard University, Boston, 1970.

Breton, A., The Economic Theory of Representative Government, Aldine Treatises in Modern Economics, Aldine Publishing Company.

Brown, C.V. and P.M. Jackson, Public Sector Economics, Martin Robertson, Oxford, 1982.

Buchanan, J.M. and G. Tullock, The Calculus of Consent, University of Michigan Press, Ann Arbor, Mich., 1962.

Buchanan, I. and R. Tollison (eds.), The Theory of Public Choice: II, University of Michigan Press, Ann Arbor, 1984.

Burgelman, R.A., Managing Innovation Systems, A Study of the Process of Internal Corporate Venturing, Unpublished doctoral dissertation, Graduate School of Arts and Sciences, Columbia University, 1980.

Carter, E., The Behavioural Theory of the Firm and Top-Level Corporate Decisions, in Administrative Science Quarterly, Vol. 16, No. 4, 1971.

Caves, Richard E., Industrial Organization, Corporate Strategy and Structure, Journal of Economic Literature, Vol. 18, March 1980.

Chandler, Alfred D., Jr., Strategy and Structure : Chapters in the History of Industural Enterprise, M.I.T. Press, Cambridge, 1962.

Child, J., Strategies of Control and Organizational Behaviour, in Administrative Science Quarterly, Vol. 8, March 1973.

Cohen, M., J.G. March and J.P. Olson, A Garbage Can Model of Organizational Choice, in Administrative Science Quarterly, Vol. 17, No. 2, 1972.

Crew, M.A., M.W. Jones-Lee and C.K. Rowley, X-Theory versus Management Discretion Theory , in Southern Economic Journal, Vol. 38, No. 2, 1971.

Dasgupta, P., S.A. Marglin and S.K. Sen, U.N.I.D.O. Guidelines for Project Evaluation, United Nations, 1972.

Downs, A., Inside Bureaucracy, Boston, Mass., Little Brown, 1967.

Earl, P., The Corporate Imagination, How Big Companies Make Mistakes, M.E. Sharper Armonk, New York, 1984.

Fischhoff, B., P. Slovic, S. Lichtenstein and R. Keeney, Acceptable Risk, Cambridge University Press, New York, 1981.

Galbraith, John Kenneth, The New Industrial State, Houghton Mifflin, Boston, 1967.

Imboden, N., A Management Approach to Project Appraisal and Evaluation with Special Reference to Non-Directly Productive Projects, Development Centre of the Organizaton for Economic Cooperation and

Development, Paris, 1978.

Jackson, P.M., The Political Economy of Bureaucracy, Totowa, Barnes and Noble, 1983.

Jones, L.R. and F. Thompson, Risk for Efficiency: Comprehensive Reform of Direct Regulation, Academy of Management Review, Vol. 9, No 4, 1984.

Leibenstein, H., Beyond Economic Man, A New Foundation for Microeconomics, Harvard University Press, Cambridge, Mass. and London, England, 1976.

Leibenstein, H., On Bulls-Eye-Painting Economics, in Journal of Post Keynesian Economics, Vol. 4, No. 3, 1982.

Lindsay, C.M., A Theory of Government Enterprise, in Journal of Political Economy, Vol. 84, No. 5, 1976

Linstone, H.A., Multiple Perspectives for Decision Making, Bridging the Gap between Analysis and Action, North-Holland, New York, Amsterdam, Oxford, 1984.

Little, I.M.D. and J.A. Mirrlees, Manual of Industrial Project Analysis in Developing Countries, Vol. II, Social Cost-Benefit Analysis, O.E.C.D., Paris, 1969.

Loasby, B.J., Choice, Complexity and Ignorance, An Enquiry into Economic Theory and the Practice of Decision Making, Cambridge University Press, Cambridge, Londen, New York, Melbourne, 1976.

Maass, A., Muddy Waters, Harvard Univerrsity Press, Cambridge, Mass., 1951.

Marris, R., The Economic Theory of Managerial Capitalism, Free Press, New York, 1964.

McCain, R.A., Competition, Information, Redundancy, X-Efficiency and the Cybernetics of the Firm, in Kyklos,Vol. 28, Fasc. 2, 1975.

McGuinness, N. and A. Conway, World Product Mandates: The Need for Directed Search Strategies, in H. Etemad and L.S. Dulude (eds.), Managing the Multinational Subsidiary, Croom Helm, London, 1986.

Mintzberg, H., The Structure of Organizations, Prentice-Hall, Englewood Cliffs, 1979.

Mintzberg, H., Power In and Around Organizations, Prentice-Hall,

Englewood Cliffs, 1983.

Mintzberg, H. and A. McHugh, Strategy Formation in an Adhocracy, Administrative Science Quarterly, Vol. 30, No. 2, June 1985, p. 160-197.

Mintzberg, H., D. Raisinghani and A. Theoret, The Structure of 'Unstructured' Decision Processes, in Administrative Science Quarterly, Vol. 21, No. 2, 1976.

Mueller, D.C., Public Choice, Cambridge Surveys of Economic Literature, Cambridge University Press, Cambridge, London, New York, Melbourne, 1979.

Murelius, O., An Institutional Approach to Project Analysis in Developing Countries, Development Centre Studies, O.C.D.E., Paris, 1981.

Niskanen, W.A., Bureaucrats and Politicians, in Journal of Law and Economics, Vol. 18, 1975.

Olson, M., The Logic of Collective Action, Public Goods and the Theory of Groups, Harvard University Press, Cambridge, Mass., 1965.

Ouchi, W.G., The Relationship Between Organizational Structure and Organizational Control, in Administrative Science Quarterly, Vol. 22, March 1977.

Pattanaik, P.K. and M. Salles (ed.), Social Choice and Welfare, Contributions to Economic Analysis, North-Holland, Amsterdam, New York, Oxford, 1983.

Pearce, D.W. and C.A. Nash, The Social Appraisal of Projects, A Text in Cost-Benefit Analysis, Macmillan Press, London, Basingstoke, 1981.

Peltzman, S., Towards a more general Theory of Regulation, Journal of Law and Economics, Vol. 19, 1976.

Pennings, J.M., D.J. Hickson, C.A. Hinings, C.D. Lee and R.E. Schneck, Uncertainty and Power in Organizations: A Strategic Contingency Model of Sub-Unit Functioning, Paper prepared for a Conference on Problems of Research on Organizational Sub-Unit Functioning, at the University of Alberta, Canada, March 1969.

Perrow, C., The Analysis of Goals in Complex Organizations, in American Sociological Review, Volume 26, 1961.

Schenker, E. and M. Bunamo, A Study of the Corps of Engineers' Regional Pattern of Investments, in Southern Economic Journal, Vol. 39,

No. 4, April 1973.

Schwenk, C.R., Cognitive Simplification Processes in Strategic Decision-making, in Strategic Management Journal, Vol. 5, No. 2, 1984.

Simon, H.A., Models of Man: Social and Rational, New York, Wiley, 1957.

Simon, H.A., Applying Information Technology to Organization Design, Public Administration Review, Vol. 33, May-June 1973.

Staw, B.M., The Escalation of Commitment to a Course of Action, in Academy of Management Review, Vol. 6, No. 4, 1981.

Stewart, F., Social Cost-Benefit Analysis in Practice: Some Reflections in the Light of Case Studies Using Little Mirrlees Techniques, in World Development, Vol. 6, No. 2, 1987.

Sugden, R., The Political Economy of Public Choice, Martin Robertson, Oxford, 1981.

Thomas, H., Strategic Decision Analysis: Applied Decision Analysis and its Role in the Strategic Management Process, in Strategic Management Journal, Vol. 5, No. 2, 1981.

Thompson, J.D., Organizations in Action, McGraw-Hill, New York, 1967.

Tullock, G., The Politics of Bureaucracy, Public Affairs Press, Washington, D.C., 1965.

Van Cauwenbergh, A. and K. Cool, Strategic Management in a New Framework, in Strategic Management Journal, Vol. 3, No. 3, 1982.

Vancil, R.F. and C.H. Green, How C.E.O.'s Use Top Management Committees, in Harvard Business Review, Vol. 62, No. 1, 1984.

Vancil, R.F. and P. Lorange, Strategic Planning in Diversified Companies, in Harvard Business Review, Vol. 53, No. 1, 1975.

Verbeke, A., Rationele Objectieven, Structurele Ineffectiviteit en Commitment in het Belgisch Zeehavenbeleid, een Multipele Perspectieven Benadering voor het Strategisch Investeringsbeleid in Complexe Organisaties, Antwerpse Lloyd, Antwerpen, 1986.

Weick, C.E., The Social Psychology of Organizing, Addison Wesley, Reading, Mass., 1979.

Williams, A., Cost Benefit Analysis : Bastard Science and or Insidious Poison in the Body Politic?, in Journal of Public Economics, No. 1, 1972.

Williamson, O.E., The Economics of Discretionary Behavior, Managerial Objectives in a Theory of the Firm, Prentice Hall, Englewood Cliffs, 1964.

Williamson, O.E., Markets and Hierarchies : Analysis and Antitrust Implications : A Study in the Economics of Internal Organization, Free Press, New York, 1975.

Williamson, O.E., The Economic Institutions of Capitalism, Free Press, New York, 1985.

Author Index

Subject index

adaptive expectations 94

administrative level 116, 117, 118, 120, 121, 122, 124

à fonds perdus 4, 5, 105, 107, 112, 114, 137

atomistic markets 9

bargaining 9, 23, 35, 71, 125

benefit-cost ratio 110

bounded rationality 5, 111, 112, 120, 121, 122, 126, 127, 128, 129

bureaucrat 2, 5, 12, 15, 17, 20, 21, 22, 25, 28, 30, 31, 34, 46, 49, 51, 96, 98, 107, 108, 117, 136

bureaucratic behaviour 22

campaign spending 18

capitalist class 68, 71

cash limits 83, 85, 86, 99, 100

civic duty fulfillment 13

class conflicts 88, 96

clientelism 50

coalition formation 18, 19, 20, 23, 47

coalition government 17, 19, 29, 30, 50

commitment model 5, 107, 113, 115, 134, 135, 138

comparative institutional assessment 110, 111

complex interest function 34

constitutional economics 36

constitutional rules 94

cost-benefit analysis 5, 105, 106, 110, 125, 127, 138

cultural system 118

distributional coalition 24

econometrics 12

economic analysis 2, 10

egoistic voter behaviour 64

election modalities 47

encompassing organization 23

ex-ante economic policy 75

expected profitability 105

factions 50

free-rider 14, 18, 23

fundamental behavioural hypothesis 11

game-theoretical model 29

game theory 12, 19, 35

goals achievement 108, 111, 112, 126

global goals 111

ideological goals 27, 28, 46

inertia 5, 128, 130, 131

inflation 62, 64, 67, 71, 72, 73, 74, 75

infrastructure investment 105, 107